Lively BIBLE LESSONS for MOPPETS

Mothers of Preschoolers
www.mops.org

Incredible things will happen™
Loveland, Colorado
group.com

Group resources actually work!

This Group resource incorporates our R.E.A.L. approach to ministry. It reinforces a growing friendship with Jesus, encourages long-term learning, and results in life transformation, because it's

Relational
Learner-to-learner interaction enhances learning and builds Christian friendships.

Experiential
What learners experience through discussion and action sticks with them up to 9 times longer than what they simply hear or read.

Applicable
The aim of Christian education is to equip learners to be both hearers and doers of God's Word.

Learner-based
Learners understand and retain more when the learning process takes into consideration how they learn best.

Lively Bible Lessons for MOPPETS

Copyright © 2007 Group Publishing, Inc.

All rights reserved. No part of this book may be reproduced in any manner whatsoever without prior written permission from the publisher, except where noted in the text and in the case of brief quotations embodied in critical articles and reviews. For information, e-mail Permissions at inforights@group.com or write Permissions, Group Publishing, Inc., Product Support Services Dept., P.O. Box 481, Loveland, CO 80539.

Visit our Web site: **group.com**

Credits

Chief Creative Officer: Joani Schultz
Senior Product Developer Children's Ministry: Patty Smith
Children's Ministry Champion: Christine Yount Jones
Authors: Karen M. Ball, Patti Chromey, Nanette Goings, Jerayne Gray-Reneberg, Ray and Cindy Peppers, Jolene L. Roehlkepartain, Amy Weaver, Jane P. Wilke, Paul Woods, and Christine Yount Jones
Editors: Cindy S. Hansen, Mikal Keefer, and Jan Kershner
Copy Editor: Dena Twinem
Art Director: Andrea Filer
Print Production Artist: Steven Plummer, Bethany Press
Cover Art Director/Designer: Andrea Filer
Illustrator: Helen H. Harrison
Production Manager: DeAnne Lear

Unless otherwise indicated, all Scripture quotations are taken from the *Holy Bible*, New Living Translation, copyright © 1996, 2004. Used by permission of Tyndale House Publishers, Inc., Carol Stream, Illinois 60188. All rights reserved.

Library of Congress Cataloging-in-Publication Data
Lively Bible lessons for MOPPETS. -- 1st American pbk. ed.
    p. cm.
ISBN-13: 978-0-7644-3573-7
(pbk. : alk. paper) 1. Bible--Study and teaching (Preschool) 2. Christian education of preschool children. I. Group Publishing. II. MOPS International, Inc.
BS600.3.L58   2007
268'.432--dc22
                                                      2007016363
10 9 8 7 6 5 4 3 2   16 15 14 13 12 11 10 09 08
Printed in the United States of America.

Table of Contents

Introduction 5

Part 1: A Lively Look at Myself

What Can I Do? 9
   Honor God by doing what he asks.

Green With Envy 14
   Give thanks for what we have and for what others have.

Frightening Fears 19
   See that God is bigger than fears. God takes care of us.

What Makes Me Special? .... .24
   Celebrate our uniqueness.

Part 2: A Lively Look at My Relationships

Friends Forever 31
   A little bit of love goes a long way in friendship.

Being Kind 36
   Understand the importance of kindness and practice it.

Learning to Share .... .42
   Learn to share our gifts.

Lend a Helping Hand. .... .47
   Reach out to people who are hurting.

Caring for God's World .... .52
   See, feel, hear, taste, and smell God's world.

Part 3: A Lively Look at My Faith

Who Is God? 61
Learn about God's love, care, and gifts.

Who Is Jesus? 67
Discover Jesus is with us wherever we go.

Talking to God 72
Know God hears and answers prayers.

God's Gift—Forgiveness 79
Know Jesus forgives us and wants us to forgive others.

Heaven: Home, Sweet Home 84
Talk about our home where we'll live forever with God.

Part 4: A Lively Look at Celebrations

A Birthday Bonanza 91
Celebrate our birthdays. Learn the bigger we grow, the more we know.

The Reason for Easter 96
Focus on the real reason for Easter—Jesus.

A Thankful Thanksgiving 102
Have fun thanking God for his gifts.

Christmas Celebration 107
Compare baby Jesus to babies we know. Celebrate his birth.

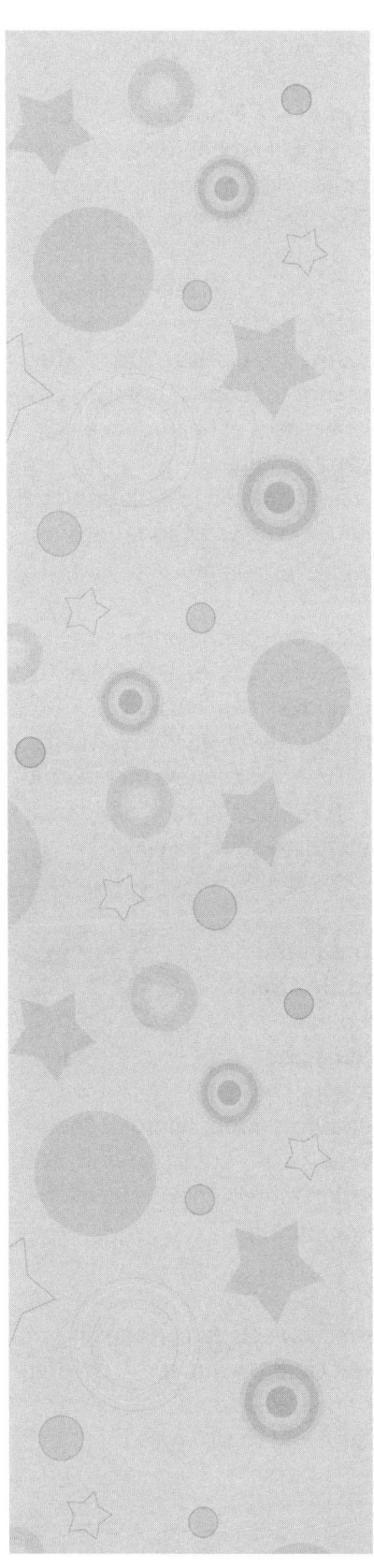

Introduction

Welcome to a resource filled with lively, active Bible lessons for preschool children ages 3 to 5. Here are fun sessions that'll hold your kids' attention and teach self-esteem-building, friendship-boosting, faith-developing topics.

Lively Bible Lessons for MOPPETS offers 18 simple-to-follow lessons that combine lively learning, colorful art projects, and scrumptious snacks.

This book is divided into these four parts:

- **Part 1: A Lively Look at Myself**—Preschoolers are growing and facing new experiences daily. This section covers topics that help young children with fear, responsibility, envy, and self-esteem.
- **Part 2: A Lively Look at My Relationships**—This section helps preschoolers look past themselves to others. Topics include kindness, helping those who are hurting, sharing, friendship, feelings, and caring for God's world.
- **Part 3: A Lively Look at My Faith**—Preschool children are interested in God, the church, and their developing faith. Faith-building topics include heaven, prayer, God's love, forgiveness, and more about God and his Son, Jesus.
- **Part 4: A Lively Look at Celebrations**—People of all ages love to celebrate special occasions. This section offers Bible lessons and celebrations for birthdays, Easter, Thanksgiving, and Christmas.

The Lively Bible Lessons

The lessons in *Lively Bible Lessons for MOPPETS* contain fast-paced activities for young children with short attention spans. The lessons include the following elements:
- **Introduction**—One or two paragraphs that introduce the lesson's topic.
- **A Powerful Purpose**—A short statement of the lesson's objective. The purpose tells you what your children will learn.

- **A Look at the Lesson**—An outline including activity titles.
- **A Sprinkling of Supplies**—A list of all items you'll need for the lesson. You'll probably want to keep a few general supplies in your room: crayons, paper, paints, newspapers, old shirts for paint aprons, pencils, and tape.
- **The Lively Lesson**—Quick, active, reflective, Scripture-based activities. Lessons start with an opening experience to set the mood for the lesson. Kids experience the topics through active learning, using their senses of hearing, seeing, smelling, tasting, and feeling.

  Lessons include participation in Bible stories, action-packed memory verses, action songs to familiar tunes, art projects, games, snacks, and more!
- **Handouts**—All lessons come with handouts. They're easy to use and you have permission to photocopy them for local church use.

  Enjoy *Lively Bible Lessons for MOPPETS*. Watch kids develop self-esteem, meet new friends, and grow in their faith. Have fun teaching Bible topics in an active, lively, and meaningful way!

Allergy Alert!

Many of the lessons in this book involve food. Be aware that some children have food allergies that can be dangerous. Know your children, and consult with parents about allergies their children may have. Also be sure to carefully read food labels, as hidden ingredients can cause allergy-related problems.

Choking Hazards!

Be aware that small objects can be choking hazards for younger children. Supervise children as they work with small objects such as raisins, dry cereal and beans, and wiggly eyes.

PART 1:

A Lively Look at Myself

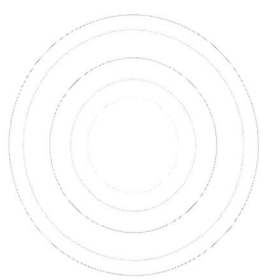

What Can I Do?

A Powerful Purpose
Preschool children will understand why it's important to do our part for God.

A Sprinkling of Supplies

- ☐ Bible
- ☐ bedsheet
- ☐ ribbon
- ☐ several colors of yarn
- ☐ crayons
- ☐ glue
- ☐ hole punch
- ☐ photocopies of the handout (p. 13)
- ☐ paper plates
- ☐ marker
- ☐ crayons
- ☐ scissors
- ☐ poster board
- ☐ brads
- ☐ resealable sandwich bags
- ☐ raisins
- ☐ M&M's candies
- ☐ pretzels
- ☐ large bowl
- ☐ napkins
- ☐ juice
- ☐ cups
- ☐ metal spoons
- ☐ pan lids

A Look at the Lesson

1. Our Band
2. Do Your Part
3. Partner Pals
4. Being Faithful
5. A Simple Song
6. Time to Do Right
7. Team Tug
8. Helping Each Other
9. Take a Bow
10. Our Part
11. Responsible Snacks

Even small children like to feel *as if they have jobs all their own, or as if they're in charge. Take advantage of children's desire to be in charge, and introduce them—in an enjoyable way—to doing good things. Help them see how they can honor God by doing what pleases him!*

The Lively Lesson

1. Our Band

(You'll need two metal spoons each for half of the children and two pan lids each for the other half.)

Greet children as they enter. Give each child either two spoons or two pan lids.

Once everyone has an "instrument," organize your band. All spoons sit together; all lids sit together. Point to the spoons and let them play their best! Motion them to stop, then point to the lids and have them play their best. Motion them to stop.

Tell band members you also want them to sing. Have them put their instruments down on the floor, then practice singing "Hallelu, Hallelu." Assign one half the "Hallelu" part and the other half the "Praise ye the Lord" part. Practice singing the song "Hallelu, Hallelu." If you don't know this song, teach kids another praise chorus you know.

After kids know the song, add instruments and make a joyful noise to the Lord. Let children sing the song and play their instruments several times. Young children learn best by repetition—plus, they love to make music! Remind children that they're praising God as they sing and play the instruments.

2. Do Your Part

Gather the instruments, then have kids sit in a circle. Say: **Everyone who sang the "Hallelu" part in the song, raise your hand.** (Pause.) **Now everyone who sang the "Praise ye the Lord" part, raise your hand.** (Pause.) **What would have happened if we reached the "Praise ye the Lord" part and no one sang? Would the song be as much fun? Let's try it and see.**

Sing the song one time through without the "Praise ye the Lord" part. Say: **That wasn't as much fun as before, was it? It was kind of confusing, too. We weren't sure when we were supposed to sing. We needed everyone to do his or her part, to be responsible. Doing what we say we'll do is important. It's like keeping a promise. What happens when you don't keep a promise?**

Listen to answers such as "People get angry; we hurt people."

Say: **God always keeps his promises to us. And he always does what he says he'll do. God wants us to follow through and do what we say we'll do. So if you say that you're going to pick up your toys at home, then it's important to do it!** Ask kids to think of other tasks they need to follow through on doing.

3. Partner Pals

Form pairs by having everyone grab the hand of someone sitting close by. Have one child in each pair close his or her eyes. Have the other child lead his or her partner around the room, making sure the child doesn't run into anything or any other person. Stress that their job is to take care of their partners.

After about a minute, have partners switch roles. Allow about another minute for them to walk around the room together.

TEACHER TIP

If some children don't want to close their eyes, let their partners lead them in walking around the room backward instead.

4. Being Faithful

(You'll need a Bible.)

Say: **Good job taking care of your partners! You did your jobs well.** Gather in a circle again.

Ask:

• **What could have happened if you hadn't led your partner carefully?**

• **Why is it important to be responsible, to do what you're supposed to?**

Say: **You did great! Your partners didn't run into anything; they were safe. You cared for your partners. You did your part. That's what God wants us to do.**

Open your Bible to Proverbs 21:3a, and show children the verse. Read this adaptation of the verse: **"Do what is right and fair."**

Say: **God is happy when we do what's right.**

Form three groups. Have one group say "Do what." Have another group say "is right." Have the third group say "and fair." Repeat until children memorize the verse. Direct the kids, having them say it softly, then gradually louder.

5. A Simple Song

Teach children this song to help them remember the Scripture verse. Sing the song to the tune of "The Farmer in the Dell."

Do what's right and fair. *(Point up with right hand.)*

Do what's right and fair. *(Point up with left hand.)*

God is happy when we all *(turn in a circle)*

Do what's right and fair. *(Wave hands in the air.)*

God helps us do what's right. *(Point up with right hand.)*

God helps us do what's fair. *(Point up with left hand.)*

God is happy when we all *(turn in a circle)*

Do what's right and fair. *(Wave hands in the air.)*

Repeat several times until children can sing the song and do the motions themselves.

6. Time to Do Right

(You'll need paper plates, a marker, crayons, scissors, poster board, and brads.)

Before class, make a clock face for each child by writing the numbers 1 through 12 around the perimeter of a paper plate. Also, cut two simple poster board arrows per child to serve as the clock hands.

Distribute the plates, and let kids color them. As kids color, go around the room and use a brad to attach the poster board arrows to the center of each plate.

After children finish coloring, gather everyone in a circle on the floor. Have them bring their "clocks." Teach children this simple rhyme:

**God wants us to do right,
Every day and night.**

Have children repeat the rhyme with you several times. Then show kids how to move the arrows on their clocks to point to different numbers. Say: **No matter what time it is, it's always the right time to do right! Let's think of ways to do what's right.**

Let each child spin his or her arrows. Tell the child what time of day the arrows indicate. Then ask everyone to think of a way to do right at that time of day or night. For example, you might say: **Your clock says it's 6 o'clock. That's the time a lot of people eat dinner. How can you do what's right at dinnertime?** Children might answer that they can help set the table, say grace, or eat their vegetables.

Make sure each child gets at least one turn to set the time, and encourage everyone to offer answers. Play several rounds as time allows. Let kids take their clocks home to remind them to do what's right all the time!

7. Team Tug

(You'll need a bedsheet.)

If the weather is nice, play this game outside on a grassy area. If not, play on soft carpet. Inside, ask kids to remove their shoes and play in their socks.

Form two teams. Twist the sheet so it's in the shape of a rope, and play Tug of War. Play at least two or three rounds.

8. Helping Each Other

Ask:
• **What was it like pulling on the sheet?**
• **Why was it hard pulling on the sheet?**

Say: **Just like it was hard to pull against another team, it's also hard to do what's right sometimes. Suppose your mom tells you to clean your room, but you want to** play? Or, what if you're supposed to help set the table for dinner, but you want to watch TV? It's not always easy to do what we're supposed to do. How can we help each other do what's right?

Listen to answers such as "Pray for each other; help each other; share; don't ask someone to play if you know he's supposed to be helping his mom." Go around the circle and, one at a time, call each child by name to say, "Do what's right."

⭐ 9. Take a Bow

Say: **I'm so glad that we can help each other do what's right. Let's play a game to celebrate!**

Have children take note of the colors they're wearing.

Say: **When I name a color, anyone wearing that color can take a bow while the rest of us clap our hands and applaud. For example, if I say, "Red!" and Tiffany and Josh are wearing red, they can bow while the rest of us clap for them.**

When everyone understands the rules of the game, call out a color. Keep calling out colors until everyone has had a chance to bow and be applauded. For extra fun, play again by calling out combinations of colors.

Say: **That was fun. Thanks for celebrating that we can help each other do what's right!**

⭐ 10. Our Part

(You'll need crayons, ribbon, different colors of yarn, glue, and photocopies of the "Our Part" handout on page 13. Cut out the face on the handout and use a hole punch to punch a hole in top.)

Give one handout and crayons to each child. Read the words on it: "Do what is right and fair." Let children draw their own faces in the circle then glue yarn on for hair. Help kids thread ribbon through the hole so they can hang the crafts at home as reminders that even though they're little, they can do what's right.

⭐ 11. Responsible Snacks

(You'll need a separate plastic sandwich bag filled with one of these items for each of your kids: M&M's candies, raisins, pretzels. You'll also need a large bowl, napkins, juice, spoon, and cups.)

Give each person a plastic bag filled with an item to make trail mix. Say: **Each of you has a part of our snack. It's your job to put your part in this big bowl.**

Ask each person to put his or her ingredient in the bowl. Say: **If someone didn't do his or her job to add to the snack, would it be as good? We each need to do our job.**

Mix the goodies and serve the trail mix on napkins. Give everyone juice to drink. Close the lesson by praying: **God, help us to do our part. Help us do what's right. Remind us to help our friends do their part, too. We love you. In Jesus' name, amen.**

Our Part

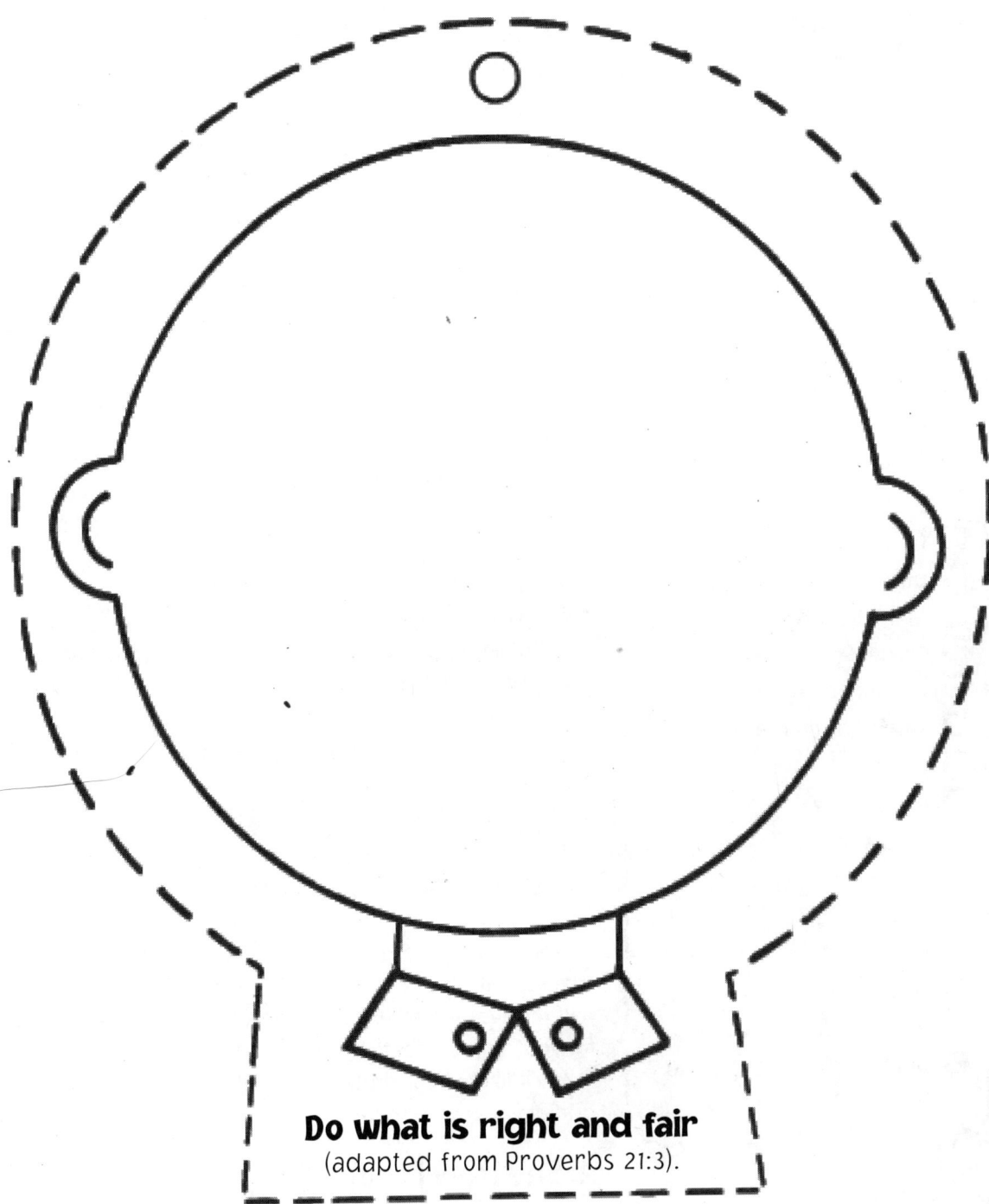

Do what is right and fair
(adapted from Proverbs 21:3).

Green With Envy

A Powerful Purpose

Preschool children will learn to be happy with the things they have, not envious of other people's things.

A Look at the Lesson

1. Look at My Snack
2. See How I Feel
3. Envious Faces
4. Flannel Board Photos
5. Good for You
6. Song of Thanks
7. Smiling Syrup
8. My Blessings
9. Spy Good Things
10. Love Is Not Envious
11. A Taste of Envy

A Sprinkling of Supplies

- ☐ Bible
- ☐ brownies
- ☐ small crackers
- ☐ paper
- ☐ marker
- ☐ flannel board
- ☐ pictures of Joseph and his special coat
- ☐ crayons
- ☐ prepared red gelatin
- ☐ small paper plates
- ☐ napkins
- ☐ table knife
- ☐ corn syrup
- ☐ food coloring
- ☐ measuring cup
- ☐ tape
- ☐ resealable plastic bag for each child
- ☐ photocopies of the handout (p. 18)

Envy is a common feeling for all people, all ages. Many adults closely watch for the newest and neatest gadgets and technology, as well as the new items their neighbors buy. Little children play with their toys but want their friends' toys.

Use this lesson to help young children deal with envy. Teach preschoolers to give thanks for what they have.

The Lively Lesson

1. Look at My Snack

(You'll need brownies and small crackers.)

When kids arrive, gather them in a circle and pass out snacks. Half of the class receives a brownie, the other half receives a cracker. Say "A brownie for you, a cracker for you" as you pass them out.

You'll likely hear protests from the cracker receivers, but just bear with them.

2. See How I Feel

(You'll need brownies and small crackers. Use a marker to draw a huge smile on a piece of paper. Draw a huge frown on another piece of paper.)

Hold up the smile paper and ask:

• **How many of you felt like this when I gave you a snack? Why?** Let kids respond with "I love brownies" or "They taste great."

Hold up the frown paper and ask:

• **How many of you felt like this? Why?** Let them respond with "I like brownies better than crackers" or "The brownie was bigger. I was hungry."

Give crackers to the children who already received brownies and brownies to the children who already received crackers. Say: **Remember, all good things come from God.**

Tell children that there's a word to describe our feelings when we want something someone else has. It's called *envy*. We feel envy when we want others' things instead of thinking of our own good gifts.

3. Envious Faces

Let everyone practice smiling and frowning. Then say: **I'm going to read some situations. If one makes you happy, show me a big smile. If one makes you feel sad, angry, or full of envy, show me a big frown.**

Read these situations:

• **Your sister just got a brand-new tricycle, and you didn't get anything.**

• **A friend is eating a juicy red apple; he gives you one, too.**

• **Your baby brother is surrounded by aunts and uncles who are oohing and aahing over him. Nobody notices you.**

• **A next-door neighbor is playing with a brand-new red truck in his brand-new sandbox. He doesn't ask you to play.**

• **You're holding your favorite book. You offer to show it to your friend.**

• **Your teacher tells you you're going to hear a good Bible story.**

4. Flannel Board Photos

(You'll need a flannel board and pictures from the story about Joseph and his special coat. Use flannel board pictures from Sunday school resources or pictures from a children's Bible or storybook. Make your own flannel board by covering a sturdy piece of cardboard—any size you want—with light-colored flannel. Glue a small piece of flannel to the back of each picture you'll use. You'll also need a Bible.)

Before you start the story, give kids a stretcher break with the following chant. Have kids follow you in doing the actions.

Smile *(stand and smile),*
Frown *(bend your knees and frown),*
Smile *(stand and smile),*
Frown *(bend your knees and frown),*
Now it's time to sit back down. *(Sit down by the flannel board.)*

Tell the story of Joseph, his special coat, and his envious brothers by reading Genesis 37:3-4, 14, 18-28. Let the children use the flannel-board pictures to help you tell the story. If time permits, tell the story again and let different children move the pictures on the board.

5. Good for You

Say: **Those brothers felt a lot of envy because Joseph's dad liked him best. Joseph got a bright-colored coat, and his brothers didn't. Sometimes we feel envy just like Joseph's brothers when we don't get what we want.**

Give kids a chance to say things that make them envious. For example, when friends get new toys and they don't. Then tell them they're going to change envy into a good feeling. Tell kids you'll stand up and say some sort of good news, then sit down. After each bit of good news, kids are to stand up and

15

say "I'm happy for you," then sit back down. Say:

• **Look! My dad just gave me a brand-new toy.**

• **My grandma is coming to take me to the zoo!**

• **My mom lets me stay up late on Friday nights.**

Add some of the situations that kids previously said made them envious. After each item you say, encourage kids to say "I'm happy for you!"

Say: **Sometimes it isn't easy to be happy for others when they get something we'd like, but that's just what God wants us to do.**

6. Song of Thanks

Say: **Let's sing a song to remind us to be happy with what God has given us. Let's thank God as we sing!** Sing the following song to the tune of "London Bridge." Have children sit in a circle and clap along to the song. Have kids stand up and shout the last line of each verse: "Thank you, God!"

**We give thanks for what we have,
What we have, what we have.
We give thanks for what we have.
Thank you, God!**

**Every good thing comes from God,
Comes from God, comes from God.
Every good thing comes from God.
Thank you, God!**

Repeat the song several times to help children learn the words.

7. Smiling Syrup

(You'll need corn syrup, measuring cup, food coloring, tape, and a resealable plastic bag for each child.)

Distribute the resealable plastic bags. Pour about ⅓ cup of corn syrup into each bag. Let each child pick a color of food coloring. Then drop a couple of drops of the chosen color into the corn syrup. Seal the bags, and then tape the seals closed. Encourage children to squish their bags until the food coloring and the corn syrup are thoroughly mixed.

Say: **God wants us to be thankful for what we have instead of sad for what we don't have.**

Encourage children to use their fingers to make a frown by tracing lightly on the outside of the bag. Review the Bible story with children. Ask them how Joseph's brothers felt when Joseph was given his colorful coat. Then remind kids that we can be happy when good things happen to other people. Remind children that God gives us all good things. Have children replace the frown with a smiley face in the syrup as they share something God has given them that makes them happy. Let children take their bags home and share the Bible story with their families.

8. My Blessings

(For each child, you'll need crayons and a copy of the "My Blessings" handout on page 18.)

Distribute the handouts to the children. Tell them each to draw a picture of a blessing—a favorite toy, pet, or somewhere nice they've been on vacation. When they finish, let them share their pictures with the others.

After each child shares, have everyone else stand up and say "I'm happy for you."

Emphasize that God blesses all of us with gifts. None of us should envy others.

9. Spy Good Things

Play a game of I Spy with children to help them recognize good things God has given them. You might say, "I spy someone with a pretty red ribbon in her hair." Encourage children to call out the name of the child with the ribbon in her hair, and then as a group say: "Let's be thankful for what we have!" Continue playing until you've spied at least one good thing for each child.

10. Love Is Not Envious

Have kids learn this memory verse adapted from 1 Corinthians 13:4: Love is kind and does not envy. Have kids repeat the verse with you using the motions. Work with them until they can say it by themselves with you just leading the motions.

Love is kind *(draw a smile on your face with both pointer fingers)*

And does not envy. *(Make a frown on your face.)*

11. A Taste of Envy

(You'll need a shallow pan of red gelatin, table knife, small paper plates, and napkins. Prepare the gelatin according to the "Jigglers" recipe on the package.)

Help children each cut a large crescent shape out of the gelatin to place on a paper plate. Have them each hold their crescent shape like a frown as you say: **God doesn't want us to be envious. It makes God sad when we envy others.**

Then have kids each hold their crescent shape like a smile. Say: **God wants us to be happy when others are happy. It makes God happy when we don't envy others. Let's gobble up any envy we may have.**

Encourage kids to gobble up their jiggly smiles.

Serve kids any leftovers.

Close with a prayer: **Thank you, God, for all our blessings. Take envy away, and make us happy for others. In Jesus' name, amen.**

My Blessings

"Love is kind and does not envy"
(1 Corinthians 13:4).

Permission to copy this handout from *Lively Bible Lessons for MOPPETS* granted for local church use.
Copyright © Group Publishing, Inc., P.O. Box 481, Loveland, CO 80539. www.group.com

Frightening Fears

A Powerful Purpose
Preschool children will recognize they don't have to be afraid because God protects them.

A Look at the Lesson

1. Don't Be Afraid
2. Fear Bubbles
3. Fears Drag You Down
4. Fear List
5. Fear Bombardment
6. Fear Protection
7. Get Rid of Those Fears
8. I'm Not Alone
9. Safe Socks
10. God Protects Us
11. God's Protective Love
12. Thanks for God's Love

A Sprinkling of Supplies

- ☐ Bible
- ☐ bubble wand and solution
- ☐ blindfold
- ☐ paper
- ☐ doll
- ☐ large box
- ☐ trash can
- ☐ unmatched socks
- ☐ markers
- ☐ dried beans or rice
- ☐ cup
- ☐ crayons
- ☐ ribbon
- ☐ stickers
- ☐ tape
- ☐ photocopies of the hand-out (p. 23)
- ☐ small box of raisins for each child
- ☐ other snacks
- ☐ canvas bag filled with heavy books

A child's world can be full of frightening things. Children don't think there's a huge, hairy, sharp-toothed monster under their bed; they know it!
Use this lesson to put fears in a new light. Let young children see they can get rid of their fears and give them to God. Help children see that God is bigger than their fears.

The Lively Lesson

1. Don't Be Afraid

(You'll need one blindfold.)

Welcome children, and tell them you're going to play a game called Don't Be Afraid.

Blindfold one child. Have the other children walk in a circle around the blindfolded child. Tell the blindfolded child to try to walk out of the circle without running into anyone. When the child is about to run into someone, yell, "Stop, kids. Don't be afraid." Then have the other children squeeze together and hug the blindfolded child. Remove the blindfold, and give it to another child to continue the game.

Say: **God tells us the same thing when we're afraid: "Stop, kids. Don't be afraid. I'm here to help you."**

2. Fear Bubbles

(You'll need a bubble wand and bubble solution.)

Say: **Sometimes when we're afraid, we just need to remember that God can help us with all of our fears.**

Explain that you'll blow some bubbles. Kids can each call out something they're afraid of, and then pop a bubble. Each time they pop a bubble, kids can say something like, "I don't have to be afraid of [scary item] because God is with me." Begin blowing bubbles. Continue blowing bubbles until children run out of fears to name.

Say: **Just as you popped the bubbles, God can pop all of our fears! We don't have to be afraid, because God loves us and will always be with us to help.**

3. Fears Drag You Down

(You'll need a canvas bag filled with heavy books—heavy enough so kids have some difficulty dragging it, but not so heavy that it causes muscle strain.)

Tell children they're going to run a short relay race that'll show them how their fears can keep them from doing their best.

Form two teams. Help teams line up at one end of the room. Give one team the heavy bag of books. Tell that team that one person at a time, team members have to drag the bag across the room and back. The other team's members can run freely. One at a time, team members each run across the room and back, and then tag the next person on their team who repeats the process. Continue until everyone has run. First team done wins.

After the first race, give the bag of books to the other team and have kids race again.

Afterward ask:

• **Which was harder—running by yourself or dragging the bag? How did you feel dragging the bag?**

Say: **Fear is like that heavy, old bag. It keeps us from doing our best, even from doing things we really want to do. Fear can keep us from doing things God wants us to do.**

4. Fear List

(You'll need a piece of paper for each child and a marker.)

Ask kids to name their fears. Some possibilities are the dark, monsters, getting lost, parents getting a divorce, or war.

Write one fear on each piece of paper. After you write one fear for each child, wad the paper and toss it to a child. Say: **[Name], grab that fear!** After each child has caught a fear, say: **Follow me to the next activity where we'll try to get rid of our fears.**

5. Fear Bombardment

(You'll need a doll, a large box, and the wads of paper "fears.")

Place a doll in the center of the room. Gather kids in a circle around it. Say: **Pretend that doll is a person who's afraid of all these fears. She's hit with them every day.**

Let kids throw their paper fears at the doll.

Next, place a large box over the doll. Ask kids to pick up a paper fear and go back to the circle. Tell them to throw the fears again and try to hit the doll.

Say: **Our fears are like these paper wads raining down on the doll. They come at us fast and hit us. But when the doll was covered by the box, the fears couldn't hit her. She was protected. God helps us like** that box helped her. He covers us with his love and protection.

6. Fear Protection

(You'll need a Bible.)

Ask: • **Who protects us from our fears?** Answers could be "God; Jesus; parents; friends."

Tell the story of David and Goliath found in 1 Samuel 17.

Say: **In the Bible, David was sometimes afraid. But he knew God would protect him. Listen to David's words.**

Read Psalm 27:1 from a children's Bible, or use this translation: **"The Lord is my light and the one who saves me. I fear no one. The Lord protects my life. I am afraid of no one." David knew that God was stronger than anything or anyone else. All we need to do is ask God to cover us—to protect us. Then the fears can't get to us. With God's help and protection, we don't need to be afraid.**

7. Get Rid of Those Fears

(You'll need the wadded paper fears and a trash can.)

Gather the paper wads of fear, unwad them, and read them aloud. After each fear you read, have kids stand and say: "I'm not afraid. God protects me." Then throw the paper fear in the trash can.

After you've thrown away all of the fears, say: **God gets rid of our fears!**

8. I'm Not Alone

Gather kids in a circle, and stand in the middle. Say: **Our family and friends also help protect us from our fears. When we're afraid, we can tell them about it. And we can ask them to pray with us. Their love** can surround and protect us. It's easier not to be afraid when we remember we're not alone.

Choose one person to come stand in the middle with you. Both of you say: **We're not alone.** Have that child choose another child to come stand in the middle with you, and all three of you say: **We're not alone.** Continue until everyone is chosen and bunched together.

9. Safe Socks

(You'll need unmatched socks, markers, a cup, and dried beans or rice.)

Set out markers and give each child a sock. Encourage children to draw things on their socks that remind them that God protects them. For example, children might draw pictures of their parents or houses. If you have mostly younger preschoolers, let them draw smiley faces on their socks to show how happy they are that God keeps them safe.

When children have finished drawing, help them to each fill their sock with a cup of dried beans or rice. Help children tie the ends of the socks tightly so nothing can fall out.

Say: **The pictures on our socks can remind us that God protects us when we're scared. Take your sock home with you, and whenever you feel scared, squeeze your "safe sock" and remember that you don't need to be scared anymore because God is with you and will help you.**

10. God Protects Us

Sing "God Protects Us" to the tune of "Frère Jacques". Encourage children to follow along as you show them the motions.

God protects us *(hide eyes behind hands)*,
God protects us.
Every day.
Every day.

You don't have to be scared *(pull hands away from eyes),*
You don't have to be scared.
God loves you. *(Hug yourself.)*
God loves you. *(Hug yourself.)*

Repeat the song several times so kids can learn the words.

11. God's Protective Love

(You'll need crayons, ribbon, tape, stickers, and other decorations. Each child will need a small, closed-up box of raisins and a photocopy of the "God's Box of Protective Love" handout on page 23.)

Tell kids they're going to decorate their own boxes to remind them that God covers them with his protective love. Give them each a box of raisins and a handout. Read the words to them: **Don't be afraid, [name]. God loves you and protects you.**

Give kids the decorating supplies. Let them color and decorate their boxes any way they want. While they're decorating, give specific words of praise as you go around to each one. Tape a handout-card to each box. Write the child's name in the space provided.

12. Thanks for God's Love

Gather in a circle, and have children show their completed boxes. Reread the handout, and have kids repeat the message after you: **Don't be afraid. God loves you and protects you.**

Pray: **Thank you, Father, for loving us and for being our protection against things that make us afraid. Help us to trust you. Help us not to be afraid. In Jesus' name, amen.**

Ask children to open their boxes. When kids find the raisins, remind them of God's protective love. Serve other snacks with the raisins. Tell kids to think about God's love every time they eat a raisin.

God's Box of Protective Love

Don't be afraid,

_____.

God loves you and protects you.

The Lord protects my life
(adapted from Psalm 27:1).

God's Box of Protective Love

Don't be afraid,

_____.

God loves you and protects you.

The Lord protects my life
(adapted from Psalm 27:1).

What Makes Me Special?

A Powerful Purpose
Preschool children will realize that each of us is special to God and to each other.

A Look at the Lesson

1. Run Around
2. Let's Make a Snowflake
3. Beach Ball Roll
4. Very Good
5. Happy-Face Stickers
6. Body Outline
7. Special to God
8. Hugging Game
9. Special Hands
10. God Says I'm Special
11. Happy-Face Snack

A Sprinkling of Supplies

- [ ] Bible
- [ ] CD of lively music
- [ ] CD player
- [ ] white paper
- [ ] pen
- [ ] safety scissors
- [ ] beach ball
- [ ] large sheets of butcher paper
- [ ] happy-face stickers
- [ ] disposable plastic container
- [ ] aluminum pie plate for each child
- [ ] spoon
- [ ] plaster of Paris
- [ ] water
- [ ] crayons
- [ ] photocopies of the handout (p. 28)
- [ ] milk
- [ ] cups
- [ ] napkins
- [ ] cookies or cupcakes with frosting happy faces

Children are unique *and wonderful. Jesus tells his disciples to "let the children come" to him. In fact, they're so special that Jesus said "the Kingdom of Heaven belongs to those who are like these children" (Matthew 19:14).*

Use this lesson to celebrate how God has made each of us special and unique. Reassure children that God's love for them is unlimited.

The Lively Lesson

1. Run Around

(You'll need a soundtrack of lively music and a CD player.)

Have children jog around the room as you play music. Have children freeze where they are and all call out their names at the same time when you stop the music. Choose a child to join you and help you stop the music. Then have everyone else clap for the child. Then he or she rejoins the game.

Start the music again, and keep going in this manner until each child has joined you and been applauded. Vary the game by changing the actions kids do to the music. Have them skip, hop, walk, and tiptoe.

Say: **You all are special. You played a fun game and clapped for each other. We're going to learn more about what makes us special and wonderful creations.**

2. Let's Make a Snowflake

(For each child, fold one square piece of white paper in half from top to bottom, in half again from side to side, then in half diagonally to form a triangle. Each child will need a pair of safety scissors. You'll also need a pen.)

Ask children to sit in a circle. Say: **Each of us is special. There's no one else like us anywhere in the world. Even people who look alike, such as identical twins, are different inside. We're like snowflakes. Did you know that no two snowflakes are alike? Let's make some snowflakes and check that out.**

Give children folded paper and safety scissors. Show them how to make snowflakes by cutting small pieces away from the outside edges. You may need to help children make their cuts. Then have kids open to reveal their snowflakes. Compare kids' snowflakes to see if any are alike. Put each child's name on his or her snowflake.

Then play a quick game. Ask children to see how quickly they can clean up all the extra bits of "snow" from the floor!

3. Beach Ball Roll

(You'll need a beach ball.)

Say: **Just like the snowflakes, we're all different. We all have things that make us special.**

Ask: • **What are some things that make us special?**

Talk about things we can *do* such as singing, playing, smiling, laughing, praying, or helping; things that we *are* such as children, daughters, sons, cheerful, smart, or helpful; even physical characteristics such as blue eyes, brown hair, freckles, strong, or graceful.

Go around the circle, and let each person say one thing that makes him or her special.

Say: **Let's play a game. I'll roll a ball to someone. The person who catches the ball must say one thing that makes him or her special. That person rolls the ball to someone else who does the same. We'll continue until everyone has a turn.**

Be ready to help if kids can't think of anything.

4. Very Good

(You'll need a Bible.)

Say: **God made us the way we are. He made everything on the earth. What are some of God's creations?**

Let kids respond with things such as heaven, earth, animals, sky, water, flowers, trees, and fish.

Read or tell the story of Creation from Genesis 1.

Say: **God made all of these things. After he made each one, he said it was good. And after God made people, he looked at his creation and said it was very good. God thinks we all are very special, because he made us to be like him.**

Read Genesis 1:31a from a children's Bible, or read this version: **"Then God looked over all he had made, and he saw that it was very good!"**

Ask kids to go around the room, shake each other's hands, and say, "God thinks you're very good."

5. Happy-Face Stickers

(You'll need a happy-face sticker for each person.)

Say: **We need to remind each other that we're special. What are some ways we can do that?**

Help kids think of ways such as hugging, kissing, saying thank you, giving a gift, doing something nice for a person.

Divide into pairs by saying: **I'll count to three. In those three seconds you have to grab the hand of someone who's standing close by you. But you can only hold one other hand. Ready? One, two, three. Got a partner?**

Give each child a happy-face sticker. Have each child put the sticker on his or her partner's hand and say, "Smile, you're special!"

6. Body Outline

(You'll need large sheets of butcher paper, crayons, and safety scissors.)

Have children lay on their backs on sheets of butcher paper. Use a crayon to trace the outlines of their bodies. Then allow children to color in their outlines by drawing clothes and facial features. If you have time, allow children to cut loosely around their outlines. As kids color, continue to remind them that each outline will look different because God made each of us uniquely special.

7. Special to God

Sing this song with the children in your class to the tune of "The Mulberry Bush."

You are special to God and me *(point to another child),*

God and me, God and me. *(Point to other children.)*

You are special to God and me. *(Point to another child.)*

God made you special. *(Clap hands.)*

Encourage children to repeat the song until they can sing it themselves.

8. Hugging Game

(You'll need a CD of lively music and a CD player.)

Ask children to stand in a circle, facing inward. Play the lively music. Have one child walk around the outside of the circle, gently patting each child on the back as he or she passes, until the music stops. When the music stops, have the child hug the person he or she is behind and say, "You're special." Then have those two children switch places and continue the game.

Let each person have a chance to walk around the circle. Play until each person has been hugged at least once.

9. Special Hands

(You'll need a disposable plastic container to mix the plaster in, an aluminum pie plate for each child, plaster of Paris, a spoon, and water.)

Say: **God made each of us special. See the lines and markings on your fingertips and the palms of your hands? There are no other hands in the whole world that have those exact same markings. God made you special! Let's make something to help us remember that God made each of us special.**

> **TEACHER TIP**
>
> Make sure to cover children's clothes with paint smocks or old T-shirts, and keep hand-washing supplies handy for cleanup afterward.

Mix a small amount of plaster of Paris with water in a disposable plastic container. (The plaster should be stiff but creamy.) Pour the plaster into the aluminum pie plates. Have children each push a hand gently into the plaster to make an impression.

Remind children that God made each of them special and different from everyone else. Let children take their handprints home in the aluminum pie plates. (The plaster will be completely dry in about a day.)

10. God Says I'm Special

(You'll need crayons and copies of the "God Says I'm Special" handout from page 28.)

Give each child a handout and crayons. Say: **This handout says "God Says I'm Special" across the top. There's space for you to draw a picture of yourself. The words say "Just like snowflakes, God made me and I'm special." Genesis 1:31 is written on the bottom. Remember, God created people and said they were very good—and very special!**

Let kids draw their pictures. If you want, you could take kids' pictures with an instant-print camera and place them on the handout instead of having kids draw.

11. Happy-Face Snack

(For each child, you'll need a cookie or cupcake with a frosting happy face on it. You'll also need milk, cups, and napkins.)

Serve the happy-face snack. Before kids eat, pray: **God, thanks for making us special. Help us remember how much you love us and how special that makes us. In Jesus' name, amen.**

Have children take the pictures and snowflakes home, or post them on a bulletin board titled "God's Special Creations." Remind kids to take home their plaster handprints.

God Says I'm Special

Just like snowflakes,
God made me and I'm special!

"Then God looked over all he had made,
and he saw that it was very good!"
(Genesis 1:31a)

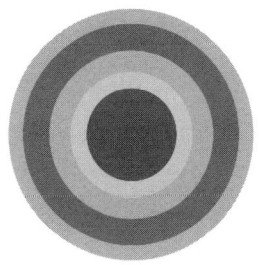

PART 2:

A Lively Look at My Relationships

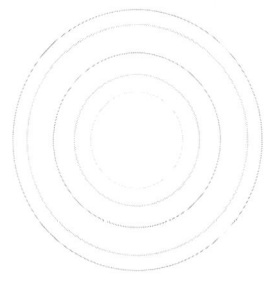

Friends Forever

A Powerful Purpose
Preschool children will learn that everybody can be a friend.

A Look at the Lesson

1. Yarn Maze
2. Beanbag Catch
3. Will You Be My Friend?
4. Good News About Friends
5. Friendship Sing-Along
6. A Whale of a Friend
7. Friendship Actions
8. Fantastic Friendship
9. Thumbody's Friend
10. Happy Faces
11. Straw Friends
12. Cheer, Cheer, Cheerios!
13. Friendship Prayer

A Sprinkling of Supplies

- [ ] Bible
- [ ] yarn
- [ ] tape
- [ ] crayons
- [ ] paper
- [ ] beanbag
- [ ] red and pink construction paper
- [ ] scissors
- [ ] poster board
- [ ] pennies
- [ ] string
- [ ] magazines
- [ ] straws
- [ ] safety scissors
- [ ] photocopies of the handout (p. 35)
- [ ] Cheerios (your choice of flavor)
- [ ] juice
- [ ] napkins
- [ ] cups

As preschool children progress, their social development changes. According to Mary Irene Flanagan, author of the *Preschool Handbook*, 3-year-olds like being with other children but still like to play alone. Four-year-olds begin to show a growing interest in doing things with other children. And by the time children turn 5, they seek affection from their peers and like to play in small groups. As preschool children develop socially, they need to understand the importance of friendship. Use this lesson to help preschoolers learn how to be a friend.

The Lively Lesson

1. Yarn Maze

(You'll need yarn and tape.)

Before class, use yarn to set up a maze in your classroom. Tape a piece of yarn to the wall and then crisscross the yarn (about waist high for children) around the room to make a path from one side of the room to the other. Include simple twists and turns by taping the yarn to chairs and tables. Children will follow the yarn like a path.

Say: **Today we're learning about how to be good friends. I want each of you to be a good friend as you help each other through this maze.**

Have children find partners, and help them go through the maze in pairs. Encourage them by telling them what good friends they are by helping their friends through the maze.

2. Beanbag Catch

(You'll need a beanbag.)

Have children sit in a circle. Give one child a beanbag, and tell the child to say his or her name before saying "is a friend." The child then gently tosses the beanbag to another child in the circle, who says his or her name before saying "is a friend" and tosses the beanbag to another child. For example, if Steven gets the beanbag first, he says, "Steven is a friend" and tosses it to Janie, who says, "Janie is a friend" before tossing it to another child.

After playing the game several times, say: **Each one of us is a friend. And now we're going to say that the other children here are friends, too.**

Play the game again only change the game by having the child say the name of the person he or she tosses the beanbag to instead of his or her own name. For example, if Steven gets the beanbag first, he says, "Janie is a friend" before tossing the beanbag to her.

After the game, say: **Isn't it great that we're all friends? God is happy when we're all good friends.**

3. Will You Be My Friend?

Encourage children to sing this song with you to the tune of "Do Your Ears Hang Low?" As children sing, have them move around the room and shake hands with someone each time they sing a new line. Continue singing until children have a chance to shake everyone's hands.

**Will you be my friend?
Will you help me pick up toys?
Will you sing a song
With the other girls and boys?
Will you be my friend
When you're happy or you're sad?
Will you be my friend?**

4. Good News About Friends

Say: **The Bible has some good news about friends. In Proverbs 17:17 it says, "A friend loves you all the time."**

Have children crouch down near the floor. Explain that they'll say the verse five times, first in a whisper and then a little louder each time. Each time they say the verse, they should stand a little taller and say it a little louder.

Then have children pat each other on the back as they say the verse one more time.

5. Friendship Sing-Along

Have children sing together these words to the tune of "Skip to My Lou." Ask children to point to themselves when they refer to themselves in the song and point to another child when singing "you." Join hands on the last line.

**I'm a friend and that is true.
I'm a friend and that is true.
I'm a friend and that is true.
I'm a friend forever.

You're a friend and that is true.
You're a friend and that is true.**

You're a friend and that is true.
You're a friend forever.

I'm a friend and so are you.
I'm a friend and so are you.
I'm a friend and so are you.
Let's be friends together.

Repeat the song several times until children know the words.

6. A Whale of a Friend

(Cut out hearts from red and pink construction paper. Cut enough hearts so each child has one. Fold all the hearts in half as shown on page 34. You'll also need crayons.)

Give the children crayons and the hearts you cut from red and pink construction paper. Be sure the hearts are folded in half so they look like whales. Tell the children to decorate their whales by adding faces. After children finish, have them exchange whales with someone in the room.

Say: **We can have a whale of a good time when we're with good friends. Now open your whales, what do you see?** (Children will see a heart.) **When we're friends, we love each other. And God wants us to be friends. Keep your whale-heart as a reminder of what good friends you have.**

7. Friendship Actions

Have children do the following actions while you read this short action story.

Everybody is a friend, and good friends stand proud. Have children stand.

The reason we can be proud is that God made us. Let's all shout, "Thank you for making us, God." Have children say, "Thank you for making us, God!"

God wants us each to be a friend. And one way we can be a friend is by smiling at the people around us. Have children smile at each other.

And by telling other people that they're good friends. Have children say, "You're a good friend" to the children around them.

Friends like to be together. They clap because they're happy. Have children clap.

They hug each other because they like each other. Have children hug each other.

And they jump for joy because everybody's a friend. Have children jump.

All this is because God made us to be good friends to each other. Let's thank God again for making us, and let's clap, too! Have children say, "Thanks for making us, God!" and clap at the same time.

Repeat the story several times.

8. Fantastic Friendship

Have children sit. Briefly tell the story of Jonathan and David from 1 Samuel 19:1-6.

Ask: • **How was Jonathan a good friend to David?**

Say: **We're going to repeat the Bible verse from Proverbs about friendship. I'll start out the sentence, and if you remember how it ends, jump up and finish the sentence.**

A friend loves you all the _____.

Continue to repeat the verse by leaving out one more word at the end of each line until the children know the verse well.

9. Thumbody's Friend

Have children hold their thumbs up. Tell them to run around the room and press their thumbs against other children's thumbs and say, "I'm thumbody's friend, and that thumbody is you!"

Let the children continue this exercise until they've each interacted with all of the other children.

10. Happy Faces

(Tape pennies and string on a piece of poster board as shown in the "Penny Face" diagram. The pennies form the eyes and noses; the string forms the face outlines and smiles. You'll also need paper and crayons.)

Give each child a piece of paper and crayon. Have children each take turns putting their piece of paper on your poster board items and rubbing gently with their crayons until the outlines and textures appear.

Ask: • **What do you see?**
• **Why are these faces happy?**

Say: **On our papers we see two happy faces. This is how friends look when they are together. They smile a lot. They laugh. They're happy. We can be happy like this when we're with our friends.**

11. Straw Friends

(You'll need magazines, drinking straws, safety scissors, tape, crayons, and photocopies of the "Friends on Stage" handout on page 35.)

Set out magazines. Encourage children to cut out people or animals from the magazines and tape the shapes to straws to create simple puppets.

Give each child a copy of the "Friends on Stage" handout. Have children color the border of the handout, then show children how to cut out the center of the handout to create a miniature stage for their straw friends.

Encourage children to form pairs and play-act for their friends using the puppets and paper stages. One child will need to hold the stage while the other child plays with the puppets. As they play with their straw friends, ask children to think of ways their straw friends can be good friends to each other.

12. Cheer, Cheer, Cheerios!

(You'll need Cheerios, juice, napkins, and cups.)

Say: **Because we're happy that we have friends and that each one of us is a good friend, let's cheer three times! Then after we cheer three times, let's celebrate being friends by eating some Cheerios.**

Together cheer three times. Then serve a snack of Cheerios and juice.

13. Friendship Prayer

Ask the children to stand in a circle and link arms. Say: **God wants us to love each other and be good friends. Each one of you is special, and you're each a good friend. Now let's bow our heads and pray.**

Pray: **God, help us to love each other and be good friends. In Jesus' name, amen.**

Friends on Stage

A friend loves you all the time
(adapted from Proverbs 17:17).

Being Kind

A Powerful Purpose
Preschool children will understand the importance of kindness and practice it.

A Sprinkling of Supplies

- ☐ Bible
- ☐ crayons
- ☐ photocopies of the handouts (p. 40-41)
- ☐ scissors
- ☐ a hole punch
- ☐ yarn
- ☐ feathers
- ☐ tempera paint
- ☐ shallow pans
- ☐ paper
- ☐ paint smocks
- ☐ water table or buckets of water
- ☐ bath toys
- ☐ towels
- ☐ bananas
- ☐ juice
- ☐ cups
- ☐ napkins
- ☐ knife
- ☐ a trash can
- ☐ an animal such as a dog, cat, or rabbit
- ☐ a wire clothes hanger for each child

A Look at the Lesson

1. A Unique Guest
2. Be Kind to Animals
3. Be Kind to Others
4. Mobile Stories
5. How to Be Kind
6. Practice Time
7. Kind Play
8. Feather Painting
9. Snack Exchange
10. Partner Cleanup
11. Kindness Prayer

Kindness *is a quality many children don't have naturally. Selfishness is human nature; kindness is a fruit of the Spirit. "But the Holy Spirit produces this kind of fruit in our lives: love, joy, peace, patience, kindness, goodness, faithfulness, gentleness, and self-control" (Galatians 5:22-23a).*

When preschoolers see kindness modeled by families, friends, and teachers, they can imitate the examples. Use this lesson to model kindness to young children. Help them learn and use that important quality in their lives.

The Lively Lesson

1. A Unique Guest

(Bring a small animal—a dog, cat, or rabbit—for children to pet. Choose a calm animal that won't get scared around the children, possibly hurting them.)

As children arrive, gather in a circle. Show them the animal, and let them take turns petting it. Show children how to pet the animal—softly, gently stroking it. Explain to children that softly petting the animal is a way to show kindness to it.

Let everyone have a chance to show kindness to one of God's creations. Then have someone take the animal back to its home.

2. Be Kind to Animals

Praise the children for being kind to the animal.

Ask: • **Who made animals?**
• **Why is it important to be kind to them?**
• **Does anyone have pets at home? Tell us about your pet.**
• **How can we be kind to animals?**

Allow time for kids to talk about being kind to animals by feeding them regularly, giving them plenty to drink, brushing them, and playing with them. Say: **God made the animals. He wants us to be kind to them.**

3. Be Kind to Others

(For each child, you'll need crayons and photocopies of the "Kind Friends" handout on pages 40-41. Cut out the four pictures on the handout. You'll also need a Bible.)

Say: **God made the animals, and God also made you. God is happy when we're kind to animals. God is also happy when we're kind to each other. God wants us to be kind to others just like we were kind to the animal.**

Distribute crayons and the first picture from the "Kind Friends" handout. Briefly explain how Matthew 9:1-2, 6-8 tells us about people who were kind to their friend who couldn't walk. The friends took the paralyzed man to Jesus so Jesus could help him walk. Allow kids to color the picture.

Distribute the second picture, and explain how Jesus responded to these friends' faith. He helped the paralyzed man walk.

Give kids the third picture, and explain to children that everyone was excited because Jesus healed the man.

After children have colored the third picture, distribute the final picture and read it to the kids: **Thank you, Jesus, for the kindness of friends.**

Let children color this final picture.

4. Mobile Stories

(You'll need a hole punch. For each child, you'll need a clothes hanger and four pieces of yarn varying in length from 6 to 12 inches.)

Punch a hole in each picture from the "Kind Friends" handout, and tie a piece of yarn to it. Attach the four pictures to a clothes hanger for each child.

After kids' mobiles are finished, help them review the story. Point to the pictures and let kids tell you the story by describing the pictures.

Ask: • **Who made the people in the story?**
• **Who made us?**
• **Why do you think we should be kind to each other?**
• **How can we be kind to each other?**

Hang the mobile stories around the room so kids can see pictures of kindness throughout the rest of this lesson.

5. How to Be Kind

Sing the following song to the tune of "The Muffin Man." Once children become familiar with the words, sing the first verse to the children and have them respond with the second verse. As they sing the second verse, have them gently pat each other on the back.

**Oh, do you know how to be kind,
How to be kind, how to be kind?
Oh, do you know how to be kind,
The way God wants you to?**

**Oh, yes, I know how to be kind,
How to be kind, how to be kind.**

Oh, yes, I know how to be kind,
The way God wants me to.

Repeat the song several times.

6. Practice Time

Lead kids in making a one-two rhythm by patting their knees. Chant these words together:
**Practice time.
Practice time.
Time to practice
Being kind.**
Form pairs by having kids each face a partner. Say: **We're going to practice being kind to each other. Shake your partner's hand and say: "I like you. You're my friend."**

Allow 30 seconds for this hand-shaking time.

Say: **Now, tell your partner one thing you really like about him or her. For example: "I really like your smile. It makes me feel good." Or "I really like your laugh. It makes me happy."**

You may need to help children who have trouble thinking of what to say. Afterward, praise the children for being kind to each other.

7. Kind Play

(You'll need a water table or partially filled buckets of water, towels, and bath toys.)

Set out a water table, or place buckets partially filled with water on towels on the floor. Place a couple of bath toys in the water, and allow children time to play. (If you'd rather not use water, just use boxes of toys.) As they play, remind children to practice being kind to each other by sharing the toys and not splashing each other. Praise them for being kind!

8. Feather Painting

(You'll need feathers, tempera paint, shallow pans, paint smocks, and paper.)

Say: **One way we can be kind to each other is by being gentle.** Hand a feather to each child. **We want to give our friends feather-soft touches instead of hurtful touches.** Allow children time to gently touch each other with the feathers.

Ask: • **How does it make you feel when your friends hit you or push you down?**
• **How does it make you feel when your friends give you feather-soft touches?**

Say: **It's good to be kind and gentle with our friends. Let's make feather paintings to help us remember to be gentle with our friends.**

Have children put on paint smocks. Allow children to dip their feathers into the tempera paint and paint on the papers. (Remind children that once there is paint on the feathers that they can't use them to give their friends feather touches anymore.)

9. Snack Exchange

(For each child, you'll need a banana, a cup of juice, and a napkin. Slice each banana at the stem to make them easier for children to peel.)

Have children find partners. Give a banana to every child. Instruct kids to give their bananas to their partners and say: "This banana is for you. Eat and enjoy."

Praise the children for their kindness in giving each other their fruit. Allow time for them to eat.

Pour juice into a small cup for each child. Again, encourage children to give their drinks to their partners. Praise them as they successfully complete the exchange.

10. Partner Cleanup

(You'll need a trash can.)

Say: **You've been kind to your partners by giving them a snack. Show your kindness even more by cleaning up for them.**

Let kids gather peelings, empty cups, and napkins and throw them away.

11. Kindness Prayer

Ask partners to hold hands, bow their heads, and pray silently as you pray: **God, thank you for friends. Help us be kind to show your love to others. In Jesus' name, amen.**

Let kids take home their mobiles as reminders of the Bible story and to help them remember to be kind to others.

Kind Friends

These are scenes from the story in Matthew 9:1-2, 6-8:

Friends carrying the lame man.

Jesus healing the man.

Permission to copy this handout from *Lively Bible Lessons for MOPPETS* granted for local church use.
Copyright © Group Publishing, Inc., P.O. Box 481, Loveland, CO 80539. www.group.com

Kind Friends

Everyone's happy because he's healed.

Thank you, Jesus, for the kindness of friends.
(Matthew 9:1-2, 6-8)

Learning to Share

A Powerful Purpose
Preschool children will hear a story about Elijah, and learn how to share.

A Sprinkling of Supplies

- ☐ Bible
- ☐ modeling dough
- ☐ strawberry jam
- ☐ butter
- ☐ bread
- ☐ sandwich bags
- ☐ strawberry powdered drink mix or juice
- ☐ water
- ☐ cups
- ☐ napkins
- ☐ magazines
- ☐ glue sticks
- ☐ safety scissors
- ☐ poster board
- ☐ small ball
- ☐ photocopies of handout (p. 46)
- ☐ yarn
- ☐ hole punch
- ☐ crayons

A Look at the Lesson

1. Create a Toy
2. Create a Story
3. When We Share
4. The Bible Skit
5. Sharing a Snack With Family
6. Modeling Sharing
7. Puzzle Share
8. Sharing Game
9. Share Our Gifts
10. I Love to Share
11. Share a Prayer

Preschoolers can sometimes be terribly possessive. It's natural for children to hold on to what they have, but sharing can be learned—through patient, diligent, and consistent teaching.
Use this lesson to help kids learn to share.

The Lively Lesson

1. Create a Toy

(You'll need modeling dough.)

As children arrive, greet them and tell them that you're glad they came. Give every other child a handful of modeling dough. Tell kids with dough to each share half with someone who doesn't have any.

Tell children to form the dough into the shape of a favorite toy, such as a ball or jump-rope. Demonstrate with a handful of dough so kids see an example. While they're shaping their own toys, ask:

• **Did you like sharing your modeling dough with a friend? Why or why not?**

• **What did it feel like to give dough away?**

• **What did it feel like when someone shared the dough with you?**

Say: **Sometimes it's not fun to share. I really appreciate the way you worked together. It pleases God when we share the nice things he gives us.**

2. Create a Story

(You'll need the completed modeling dough toy shapes.)

As children complete their work, ask them to sit in a large circle. Say: **We're going to make up a story about sharing, using your dough figures. When I pause telling the story, we'll go around the circle and you'll hold up your dough figure and say what it is.**

Once upon a time, God blessed some children with all kinds of toys, such as… *(Go around the circle and have kids name their dough toy shapes.)*

One day a little girl and boy moved into town. They were very poor. They didn't have many toys. They didn't have much of anything. They didn't have… *(Go around and have kids name toys.)*

All the children of the class met the two children and decided they wanted to share their toys with them. "Here," they said. "Play with us. Play with our…" *(Go around and have kids name toys.)*

Everyone shared and was happy.

3. When We Share

Sing "When We Share" to the tune of "The Farmer in the Dell." Use this song to teach children what sharing looks like. Pick a small classroom toy to hold, and have everyone sit in a circle. Pass the object to the child on your left as you sing. Encourage children to keep passing the item and continue singing until everyone has held the item. Then choose a new item and sing and share again!

God's happy when we share.
God's happy when we share.
Hi-ho, we're sharing, oh
God's happy when we share.

4. The Bible Skit

(You'll need a Bible.)

Open your Bible to 1 Kings 17:8-16. Make sure to use a translation that's easy for the children to understand. Read the story about Elijah and the widow who shared her food.

Say: **We're going to act out this Bible story. Everybody stand up. Half of you will be Elijah, and the other half will be the widow. I'll tell you what to say and do.**

Elijah was very hungry. *(Elijah group says, "I'm very hungry.")*

He saw a woman. *(Elijah group and widow group wave to each other.)*

Elijah asked for water. *(Elijah group says, "I'm thirsty. Can I have some water?")*

The widow said, "OK." *(Widow group says, "OK" and pretends to give water.)*

Elijah asked for bread. *(Elijah group says, "Can I have some bread?")*

The widow said, "I barely have enough for my family" *(widow group says the words),*

But she did it anyway. *(Widow group says, "OK. Here.")*

And God kept the flour and oil coming and coming. *(All say, "Thank you, God!")*

The widow shared *(tell widow group to wave)*
With Elijah *(tell Elijah group to wave),*
And God blessed them both. *(Clap.)*

5. Sharing a Snack With Family

(Prepare strawberry jam and butter sandwiches. Make one sandwich for each child, and cut the sandwich in half. Place each half in a sandwich bag. You'll also need juice or strawberry powdered drink mix and water, cups, and napkins.)

Say: **When the widow shared as God wanted her to, God took care of her. Often we're afraid to share our things because we're afraid we won't have them anymore. But God will always be good to us when we're kind to others and share.**

Distribute the sandwiches, two halves for each person. Say: **Eat one now and share the other with your family when you go home.**

Give kids prepared drink mix or juice, and let them enjoy eating the snacks.

6. Modeling Sharing

(You'll need the modeling dough toys children created earlier.)

Say: **The Bible tells us in Luke 3:11 to share what we have with others. Let's say that together.**

Lead children in saying, "Share what you have with others."

Have children sit in a circle, and give each child one of the modeling dough toys. Each time children say the verse, have them pass the dough toys to the left to "share" them. Play for several minutes until kids can say the verse by themselves.

Say: **God is happy when we share what we have with others.**

Set aside the modeling dough toys.

7. Puzzle Share

(You'll need magazines, glue sticks, safety scissors, and poster board.)

Tell children they're going to make a craft to help them practice sharing. Encourage children to find a magazine picture that they like, and then show them how to cut out the entire page. Help them glue the picture to a piece of poster board. Once the glue has dried for a minute, allow them to cut the picture into five or six pieces.

Say: **Let's practice sharing by letting our friends put our new puzzles together.**

Have children form pairs, and let partners try to put each child's puzzle together. Compliment children for sharing their puzzles with their partners. Let children take their puzzles home to share with their families.

8. Sharing Game

(You'll need a small ball.)

Ask children to sit in a circle with their hands behind their backs. Have one child sit in the center of the circle, close his or her eyes, and count to 10. Hand a small ball to a child in the circle, and encourage him or her to pass it behind the back to the next child in the circle. Have children keep passing the ball until the child in the center stops counting.

Everyone will keep their hands behind their backs when the child in the center of the circle opens his or her eyes. That child will then guess who has the ball by calling out, "[Child's name], share the ball!" If that child is holding the ball, they'll trade places. If not, retrieve the ball, choose a new person for the center of the circle, and play again. Play until each child has had a turn in the center of the circle.

9. Share Our Gifts

(You'll need photocopies of the "Share Our Gifts" handout on page 46, and crayons. Cut out the bread shape from each handout and punch two holes in the top.)

Give each child crayons and a handout. Read the words. Ask kids to say them with you as you read them again: **God wants you to share.** Explain that the bread represents the bread the widow shared with Elijah in the Bible story.

Let children color their bread shapes. Say: **You've really learned your lesson well** because I see several of you sharing your crayons.

When children finish coloring, thread a piece of yarn through the holes of each bread shape and tie to make a necklace. Invite kids to share their art with their families when they get home.

10. I Love to Share

Ask kids to stand and join hands in a circle. Sing the following song to the tune of "Twinkle, Twinkle, Little Star." Go through the song slowly and teach the words and actions. Repeat it several times.

How I, how I love to share *(walk to the middle of the circle)*
With my neighbors everywhere. *(Walk out.)*
It pleases Jesus when I do. *(Kids point up.)*
It makes us happy, me and you. *(Kids shake hands with someone and join hands in a circle again.)*
How I, how I love to share *(walk to the middle of the circle)*
With my neighbors everywhere. *(Walk out.)*

11. Share a Prayer

(You'll need the modeling dough and sandwich bags.)

Ask children to stay in the circle, holding hands. Pray: **Dear God, thank you for your gifts. Help us share what we have with others. In Jesus' name, amen.**

Give each child a handful of the modeling dough in a sandwich bag to take home and share with someone else.

Share Our Gifts

God wants you to share (adapted from Luke 3:11).

Lend a Helping Hand

A Powerful Purpose

Preschool children will hear a Bible story about the good Samaritan and practice helping others.

A Sprinkling of Supplies

- [ ] Bible
- [ ] masking tape
- [ ] doll
- [ ] latex-free adhesive bandages
- [ ] elastic bandage
- [ ] wet washcloths
- [ ] towels
- [ ] pictures of the good Samaritan story
- [ ] a beanbag
- [ ] tempera paints
- [ ] foil pans
- [ ] old shirts or smocks
- [ ] cookie cutters
- [ ] photocopies of the handout (p. 51)
- [ ] napkins
- [ ] cups
- [ ] milk
- [ ] sugar cookies
- [ ] marshmallows
- [ ] pretzel sticks
- [ ] marker
- [ ] envelopes
- [ ] stamps
- [ ] resealable bags

A Look at the Lesson

1. Helpful Exercises
2. Fast First Aid
3. The Good Samaritan
4. Toss a Tale
5. Create a Card
6. I'm a Little Helper
7. Repeat-After-Me
   Prayer
8. Cookie Snack
9. Bandage Reminder
10. Don't Forget the Donkey
11. Mail a Card

Preschool children love to help. They enjoy getting along with others and want to please. Helping other people encourages interaction, reinforces biblical values, and helps model Christian behavior.

Use this lesson to teach preschoolers about helping. Give them a chance to be kind to each other.

The Lively Lesson

1. Helpful Exercises

(You'll need masking tape.)

Before this activity, place two 3-foot pieces of masking tape on the floor about a foot apart.

Say: **Today we're going to hear about someone in the Bible who helped a man who was badly hurt. We're going to learn about how important it is to help others. But before we do, we're going to *practice* helping each other as we do some fun exercises with a partner.**

Have children form pairs, and lead them through these exercises.

- **Jump the Tape:** For this exercise, have children hold hands with their partners while they try to jump from one piece of tape to the other. Allow children to continue jumping back and forth. For extra fun, move one piece of tape farther away to make it more of a challenge.

- **Row the Boat:** Have partners sit opposite each other with their legs spread apart. One child will lean in and hold his or her partner's hands and then pull upright to sit, which pulls the partner inward. Encourage children to gently pull back and forth in a seesaw motion.

- **Jumping Beans:** For this exercise, partners hold hands and begin bouncing lightly. After a bit of bouncing, they can progress to jumping up and down. Partners can also try hopping on one foot at the same time while holding each other's hands.

Say: **Wow, you did a good job helping your partner with these exercises! Let's learn more about how we can help others.**

2. Fast First Aid

(Place the following supplies on a table: a doll, adhesive bandages, an elastic bandage, wet washcloths, towels.)

Gather around the table with the doll and first-aid supplies on it. Say: **Pretend this doll is a little child and she's just been badly hurt. What could you use to help her feel better?**

Let children wipe the doll with wet washcloths, dry her off, put adhesive bandages on injuries, and wrap an arm or leg with the bandage. Then ask:
- How did we help this doll?
- Have you ever helped someone? When?
- How does it make you feel when you help someone?

3. The Good Samaritan

(You'll need a Bible.)

Say: **Jesus told stories of how other people were helpers, too. Let's read about a helper called the good Samaritan. He was a man from a country called Samaria.**

Read the story from Luke 10:30-37 in a children's Bible. Pause after each verse. Have kids say, "Jesus wants us to help" and clap as they say each word.

Then retell the story and have the children act out the different parts as you tell it. Be sure each child has a part, whether as an actor, part of the scenery, or providing sound effects.

4. Toss a Tale

(You'll need a beanbag and pictures of the good Samaritan story.)

Tell kids they're going to play a game to help them remember the story. Lay the pictures on the floor. Have children take turns tossing the beanbag on one of the pictures and telling the part of the story depicted. You go first so they see how to do it; then let them take turns tossing a tale.

For example, if a beanbag lands on a picture of a hurt man on a donkey, a child may tell about how the good Samaritan put the hurt man on his donkey and took him to get help.

5. Create a Card

(Prepare a table with card-making supplies such as tempera paint in foil pans, cookie cutters, and old shirts or smocks. Photocopy the "Create a Card" handout on page 51. Ask your pastor about congregation members who are ill or who need extra prayers and encouragement. Make a list of their names and addresses.)

Say: **Today we're going to be God's helpers, too. We're going to help people feel better. We're going to make get-well cards for people who are sick or need some cheering up.**

Help children cover their clothes with old shirts or smocks. Give them each a handout. Read the words: **God loves you so much. He's watching over you.**

Show kids how to dip a cookie cutter in the paint, lift it out, and "stamp" the handout. Tell them to design their cards any way they want—repeat the same shape with different colors or use different shapes and overlap prints.

Complete the cards.

6. I'm a Little Helper

After children wash their hands and clean up, sing the following song to the tune of "I'm a Little Teapot." Encourage children to sing and do the motions with you.

I'm a little helper, watch me go. *(Make muscles and march in place.)*

I'll be a helper from head to toe. *(Touch your head and then your toes.)*

I will help my friends and family, too. *(Stretch out one arm then the other.)*

I help because God wants me to! *(Point up, and turn in a circle.)*

7. Repeat-After-Me Prayer

While cards are still drying, ask kids to pray by repeating each line you say and the actions you do.

Dear God *(fold hands),*

We are your helpers. *(Raise hands to heaven.)*

Let us be good helpers this week *(put hands on shoulders)*

To all of those people around us. *(Motion arms all around.)*

In Jesus' name, amen. *(Fold hands.)*

8. Cookie Snack

(You'll need napkins, cups, milk, and cookies. For extra fun, make cookies before class using the cookie cutters used for the art project.)

Follow the prayer with a snack of milk and cookies. As they munch on their cookies, let children go by the table and look at the card designs everyone made.

9. Bandage Reminder

(You'll need latex-free adhesive bandages and a marker.)

Gather kids in a circle, and ask:

• **Who are God's helpers?** Name each child in the class.

• **How can we help others?**

To help remind kids of today's lesson and the fact that they are God's helpers, write "Luke 10:30-37" on an adhesive bandage for each child. Place the bandages on the backs of kids' hands. Tell kids that Luke 10:30-37 is the place in the Bible that tells about the good Samaritan. Encourage kids to ask a parent to read the story again at home.

10. Don't Forget the Donkey

(You'll need marshmallows, pretzel sticks, and resealable bags.)

Help children find partners. Distribute marshmallows and a handful of pretzel sticks to each child.

Say: **Let's make donkeys to remember how the good Samaritan put the hurt man on his donkey to take him to an inn.**

Have partners work together to create two donkeys using the pretzel sticks and marshmallows. Allow children time to figure out how to make a donkey from these supplies. If they need help, show them how to attach several marshmallows together using a pretzel stick as a connector. Then they can add four pretzel legs, a pretzel neck, and a marshmallow head.

Help kids place their donkeys in resealable bags to take home.

Say: **Take your donkey home to show your family. Use it to tell them the story of the good Samaritan.**

11. Mail a Card

(You'll need envelopes addressed to the congregation members on your list. Mark an X on each envelope where kids are to stick a stamp.)

Check to see if the get-well cards are dry. If they are, let kids each place their card in an envelope and stick a stamp in the corner over the X. Let them take their cards home to mail. Or, if time allows, take the entire class to a nearby mailbox and let kids mail their cards.

Create a Card

God loves you so much. He's watching over you.

Jesus wants us to help (adapted from Luke 10:37).

Permission to copy this handout from *Lively Bible Lessons for MOPPETS* granted for local church use.
Copyright © Group Publishing, Inc., P.O. Box 481, Loveland, CO 80539. www.group.com

Caring for God's World

A Powerful Purpose
Preschool children will learn practical ways to care for God's creation.

A Look at the Lesson

1. Puzzles—Putting It Together
2. Experience God's Creation
3. Pick a Picture
4. Let's Make a World
5. Something's Missing
6. Growing Creation
7. Care Walk
8. Earth Patrol
9. Creation Rubbings
10. Bird Feeders
11. Creation Song

A Sprinkling of Supplies

- ☐ Bible
- ☐ several simple puzzles with nature or animal pictures on them
- ☐ magazines
- ☐ catalogs
- ☐ safety scissors
- ☐ newsprint
- ☐ marker
- ☐ grass seeds
- ☐ cotton balls
- ☐ water
- ☐ resealable plastic bags
- ☐ tape
- ☐ safety pins or tape
- ☐ recycled paper
- ☐ crayons
- ☐ leaves
- ☐ paper
- ☐ O-shaped cereal
- ☐ yarn
- ☐ fruit
- ☐ photocopies of the handouts (pp. 56-57)

Children this age are naturally enthusiastic about the world around them. Animals, trees, colors, shapes, smells—everything in nature is a source of great delight.

Use this lesson as an adventure for all of the senses. Focus the children's attention on how things feel (the sun on their faces), smell (flowers), taste (things to eat), sound (birds and animals), and look (all creation around them). Use this time to help children discover the wonders of God's world and to recognize how sad we would be if we were to lose any of it.

The Lively Lesson

1. Puzzles—Putting It Together

(You'll need several simple puzzles with nature or animal pictures on them.)

Place the puzzles around on the floor. As children enter the room, invite them to put the puzzles together. Encourage kids to work together and cooperate to complete the pictures.

2. Experience God's Creation

(Do this activity outdoors. In case of bad weather, prepare an indoor nature walk. Tape pictures of flowers, the sun, streams, and animals on walls in the hall or various rooms.)

Say: **Today we're going to take a nature walk and experience God's creation. We're going to see** (point to your eyes and have kids each point to their eyes), **hear** (point to your ears and have kids each point to their ears), **smell** (point to your nose and have kids each point to their nose), **taste** (point to your mouth and have kids each point to their mouth), **and feel** (wiggle your fingers and have kids each wiggle their fingers) **God's wonderful creation.**

Go outside and:
• see the clouds, sun, trees, and seasonal gifts such as flowers.
• hear the birds, insects, and wind.
• smell the flowers and trees.
• taste a blade of grass or a gulp of fresh air.
• feel rough tree bark, smooth rocks, and the cool grass beneath your feet.

3. Pick a Picture

(You'll need magazines, catalogs, and safety scissors.)

When you come back to the room, ask children what they liked best about the nature walk. Distribute the magazines and catalogs. Let kids find nature pictures that remind them of what they liked on the walk. Help kids tear or cut out the pictures. Remind children of everything they saw, heard, smelled, tasted, and felt.

4. Let's Make a World

(Draw a large circle on a sheet of newsprint, and tape it to the wall. You also will need the pictures from the last activity.)

Say: **Our world is a beautiful place. God created it with all kinds of wonderful things! Let's make a picture of our world and put on it all the things we liked from our walk.**

Ask children to bring up the pictures they cut out and lightly tape them inside the circle. Try to include a wide variety of pictures. When you've finished, stand back, look at the "world," and have everyone say, "What a wonderful world God made!"

5. Something's Missing

Say: **God made all the things we put into our world picture. What would our world be like without them?**

Start taking photos off, one by one. After removing each one, ask children:
• **How would you feel if** [flowers, clouds, animals, lakes] **weren't in our world any more?**

When you've taken everything off, ask:
• **If all of these wonderful gifts were gone, what would the world be like?**

Listen to children's responses, such as empty, ugly, wouldn't smell as good.

6. Growing Creation

(You'll need grass seeds, cotton balls, water, and resealable plastic bags.)

Say: **Let's see what it's like to take care of a little bit of God's creation. We're going to grow some grass from these seeds.** Hold up grass seeds. **It will take a couple of days, but once they grow, you'll need to water them and take care of them, just as God wants us to take care of his world.**

Have children place some cotton balls in the bottom of their bags, and then put a little bit of water on the cotton. Let them add grass seeds. Remove the excess air in each bag and seal it.

Have children take the bags home with them and place their grass seeds in a dark place until the seeds sprout. After the seeds sprout, parents can help children transplant them into a sunny spot in the yard.

7. Care Walk

(You'll need photocopies of the "What Can I Do?" handout on page 56 and a Bible.)

Open your Bible to Genesis, and explain that it's the first book in the Bible. Read this adapted version of Genesis 1:26: **"Human beings will rule over the fish in the sea, the birds in the sky, the livestock, all the wild animals on the earth, and the small animals that scurry along the ground."** Like a parent takes care of a child he or she "rules over," we need to take care of our world.

After you read, have kids stand and say, "Let's take care of God's creation!"

Say: **There are some simple things we can do to help take care of our earth. Follow me and I'll show you.**

Take children on a Care Walk to show some of the ideas on the "What Can I Do?" handout. For example, lead kids to a light switch and read: **Turn off the lights when you leave a room.** Lead them to a water faucet and read: **Don't run the water when brushing your teeth.**

After your Care Walk, return to the room. Give kids each a photocopy of the "What Can I Do?" handout. Say: **Take this list home, and show it to your parents. Ask them to help you do at least one of these things during the next week.**

8. Earth Patrol

(You'll need photocopies of the "Earth Patrol" handout on page 57. If possible, photocopy the handout on recycled paper. Cut out the badges. You'll also need safety pins or tape and crayons.)

Give children each a badge and crayons. Read the words: **Earth Patrol.** Let children color the badges. When you pin or tape a finished badge to each child, say: **I now commission you to Earth Patrol. It's your job to keep watch and take care of the earth.**

After everyone has been commissioned, pray: **Father, thank you for this wonderful, beautiful world you have given us. Help us not to hurt it. Help us learn how to take care of it. In Jesus' name, amen.**

9. Creation Rubbings

(You'll need to pick some fresh leaves while you're on your nature walk or find some textured leaves at a craft store. You'll also need paper and crayons.)

Show children the leaves. Say: **God created beautiful leaves, and God wants us to enjoy them and take care of the trees that grow them. Let's make some crayon rubbings to remind us to always take care of God's creation.**

Set the leaves on a table. Help children each place a sheet of paper over a leaf. Then show children how to rub a crayon across the paper as a leaf impression emerges.

10. Bird Feeders

(You'll need O-shaped cereal such as Cheerios and 10-inch pieces of yarn.)

Say: **One way we can take care of God's creation is to take care of the wild animals that live near us. We're going to make bird feeders that can be hung from a tree branch or out a window. When birds come to visit your house, they'll have something good to eat.**

Give each child a length of yarn and handful of cereal. Help each child tie a knot at the end of his or her yarn, then let children thread the cereal onto the yarn. You may want to put a small piece of tape at one end of the yarn to prevent it from fraying as children thread the cereal.

As children finish, help them tie the ends of the yarn so the cereal stays in place.

11. Creation Song

Serve children a snack of fruit. Before children eat, have them sing this song to the tune of "Are You Sleeping?" Remind children that God gave us this amazing world and we need to take care of it.

Can you feel it? *(Rub hands on arms throughout verse.)*
**Can you feel it?
That warm sun,
That warm sun.
It's God's good creation.
It's God's good creation.
Oh, how fun.
Oh, how fun.**

Can you hear it? *(Put hand behind ear throughout verse.)*
**Can you hear it?
That small bird,
That small bird.
It's God's good creation.
It's God's good creation
That we heard,
That we heard.**

Can you taste it? *(Rub tummy throughout verse.)*
**Can you taste it?
That nice treat,
That nice treat.
It's God's good creation.
It's God's good creation.
God is sweet.
God is sweet.**

What Can I Do?

1. Turn off the lights when you leave a room.

2. Don't run the water when brushing your teeth. Just turn it on to wet your brush and to rinse it off.

3. Put a plastic jug filled with water in your toilet's tank so it doesn't use as much water.

4. Use a cloth towel instead of a paper towel to dry your hands.

5. Paint and draw on recycled paper.

6. Set dry bread out in your yard for the birds to eat.

7. Throw trash in trash cans, not on the ground.

8. Recycle! Newspapers, cans, bottles, plastic, cereal boxes, aluminum foil—all can be recycled.

9. Don't litter.

10. Cut the plastic rings that come on six-packs before you throw them in the trash. Small animals and birds have caught their necks in the rings.

11. Check with your local zoo to see if they have an adopt-an-animal program. Help care for all of God's creation.

They will rule over the earth
(adapted from Genesis 1:26).

Earth Patrol

Permission to copy this handout from *Lively Bible Lessons for MOPPETS* granted for local church use.
Copyright © Group Publishing, Inc., P.O. Box 481, Loveland, CO 80539. www.group.com

PART 3:

A Lively Look at My Faith

Who Is God?

A Powerful Purpose

Preschool children will learn about God and how much he loves them.

A Look at the Lesson

1. Color Their World
2. God Made the World
3. The Bible Tells Me So
4. Jesus Loves Me
5. Hugs of Love
6. God's Hug
7. He Gave Us Us
8. Animals for Us
9. God's Love Game
10. A Heart for God
11. Love Prayer

A Sprinkling of Supplies

- [ ] Bible
- [ ] crayons
- [ ] red construction paper
- [ ] glue
- [ ] 4-foot sheets of butcher paper
- [ ] scissors
- [ ] animal crackers
- [ ] milk
- [ ] cups
- [ ] photocopies of the handouts (pp. 65-66)

Preschoolers are beginning to form their ideas about who God is. Some view God as a loving parent. Others think of him as a grandfather-type. And others think of him as one who doesn't like them to do certain things. Preschoolers need their questions about God answered simply and truthfully. Use this lesson to help your preschoolers learn about God and how he loved us so much he sent us his Son, Jesus, to die for us.

The Lively Lesson

1. Color Their World

(For each child, you'll need crayons and a photocopy of the "God Made the World" handout on page 65.)

Welcome the children as they arrive. Give them each a photocopy of the "God Made the World" handout and crayons. Have them color the items on the page.

After everyone has had a chance to color, tell the kids they're going to learn about God today.

Ask: • **Who made the things you just colored?**
• **Why did God make them?**

Say: **We know God loves us, and one of the**

reasons we know that is because he made wonderful flowers, trees, and animals and gave them to us to enjoy. Let's sing a song about that.

2. God Made the World

Sing the following song to the tune of "John Jacob Jingleheimer Schmidt." As you name the different types of things God created, encourage children to act each thing out.

God made the world for you and me
Because he loves us so.
He created birds in trees
And flowers with some bees.
Oh yes,
God made the world for you and me.

God made the world for you and me
Because he loves us so.
He created playful cats
And those tiny little gnats.
Oh yes,
God made the world for you and me.

3. The Bible Tells Me So

Say: **Another reason we know God loves us is because the Bible tells us that he does.**
Help kids memorize this Bible verse: "Love comes from God" (1 John 4:7b). Use motions to convey the words to the children as you say them.
Love (wrap your arms around yourself)
Comes (motion with your hand as if signaling someone to come to you)
From God. (Point up.)
Say the verse with the children three or four times. Have them stand and do the motions with you. Then let the children try saying one word by themselves as you do the motions. After a couple of more times, they should be able to say the verse by themselves.

4. Jesus Loves Me

Say: **The Bible tells us that love comes from God. The Bible also tells us that Jesus loves us.**
Sing "Jesus Loves Me" with the children. Use these actions.
Jesus (point up)
Loves (wrap arms around yourself)
Me (point to yourself);
This I know (point to your head)
For the Bible (form a Bible with your two hands)
Tells me so. (Point to yourself.)
Little ones (motion like your hand is placed on a little child's head)
To him belong. (Point up.)
They are weak (look weak),
But he is strong. (Form strong arms.)

Yes (nod head),
Jesus (point up)
Loves (wrap arms around yourself)
Me. (Point to yourself.)
(Repeat "Yes, Jesus loves me" three times.)
The Bible (form an open Bible with your two hands)
Tells me so. (Point to yourself.)

Then say: **To remind us that God loves us, too, let's put his name in the song.**
Sing "God Loves Me" using the same actions.

5. Hugs of Love

(You'll need a Bible.)
Say: **You know what? I love you, too!** Go around and hug each child as you call him or her by name and say: [Name], **I love you.** Have kids move to a different part of the room and sit down on the floor. Then say: **I hugged you to show my love for you. God doesn't come and hug us like I hugged you. But he has shown us how much he**

loves us by sending us his Son, Jesus.

Read a children's Bible version of John 3:16 or read this: **"For God loved the world so much that he gave his one and only Son, so that everyone who believes in him will not perish but have eternal life."**

Explain that when we believe in Jesus, he'll be our best friend here on earth, and then someday we can live forever with him in heaven.

6. God's Hug

(You'll need 4-foot pieces of butcher paper, scissors, and crayons.)

Say: **Let's make a "hug" to remind us of God's love.**

Help each child find a partner. Encourage one child to lie down, with arms straight out, on the butcher paper, while the other child outlines only his or her arms. Have the children switch places so each child has a drawing. When the drawings are done, children can draw lines to connect the two arms. Help children cut out the arms, which become a hug when you wrap it around yourself. Have the children use crayons to decorate their hugging arms.

7. He Gave Us Us

Say: **Another way God shows us he loves us is by giving us bodies we can do things with. Let's stand up and thank God for the bodies he's given us.**

Have kids spread out. Tell them to repeat the words after you and follow your motions. Be sensitive to handicapped children in your class. Don't use any motions they can't do.

Thanks, God, for our hands. *(Wave hands in the air.)*

Thanks, God, for our feet. *(Wiggle a foot in the air.)*

Thanks, God, for our elbows. *(Flop your elbows out at your sides.)*

Thanks, God, for our knees. *(March with your knees going high.)*

Thanks, God, for our heads. *(Roll your head around and around.)*

Thanks, God, for our hips. *(Wiggle your hips.)*

Thanks, God, for our seats. *(Sit down on the floor in a circle.)*

8. Animals for Us

(You'll need animal crackers, milk, and cups.)

Distribute the animal crackers, and serve the milk. Before letting kids eat their crackers, go around the circle and let them describe one of their animals. Say: **Remember what we colored earlier? God loves us so much he gave us all sorts of neat things in our world. Some of those things are animals. And the milk we're drinking came from one of those animals: a cow!**

Offer a prayer thanking God for the love he showed us by giving us animals.

9. God's Love Game

Say: **Let's play a memory game to see if we can remember some of the ways God shows his love for us.**

Have children sit in a circle. Start off by saying: **"God love us. God gives us trees."** The child on your right will then repeat the statement and add something else that God gives us to show his love for us. Continue this pattern going around the circle. Help children if they forget the order, or occasionally start from the beginning and repeat what's been said.

10. A Heart for God

(You'll need glue, crayons, red hearts cut from construction paper, and the "God Loves Me"

handout on page 66. Cut the hearts so they fit over the center heart shape on the handout.)

Pass out the handouts, glue, and red paper hearts. Read the handout, and explain where to glue the hearts. Let the children glue the hearts in place and color the letters.

Ask if anyone remembers the memory verse (Love comes from God). If no one says it, say it with the children a couple of more times. Work through it until they can say it while you do just the motions.

11. Love Prayer

(You'll need the completed "God Loves Me" handouts.)

Place the "God Loves Me" handouts in the center of the room. Ask the children to form a circle around the handouts. Say: **Look at all of these reminders of God's love. Let's pray and thank him for his love.**

Pray, thanking God for showing us his love in so many ways—our bodies, animals, our world, and especially his Son, Jesus.

Then have kids place their arms on each other's shoulders and take three steps in toward the center. When they're all bunched together in a group hug, have everybody shout "God loves us!"

God Made the World

"Love comes from God" (1 John 4:7b)

Permission to copy this handout from *Lively Bible Lessons for MOPPETS* granted for local church use.
Copyright © Group Publishing, Inc., P.O. Box 481, Loveland, CO 80539. www.group.com

"Love comes from God" (1 John 4:7b).

Permission to copy this handout from *Lively Bible Lessons for MOPPETS* granted for local church use.
Copyright © Group Publishing, Inc., P.O. Box 481, Loveland, CO 80539. www.group.com

Who Is Jesus?

A Powerful Purpose

Preschool children will learn that Jesus is with them all the time.

A Sprinkling of Supplies

- ☐ Bible
- ☐ markers
- ☐ spring clothespins
- ☐ white crayons
- ☐ white construction paper
- ☐ watercolors
- ☐ different-colors of tissue paper
- ☐ glue
- ☐ paintbrushes
- ☐ old shirts or aprons
- ☐ 9x12-inch piece of construction paper
- ☐ crepe paper
- ☐ tape
- ☐ stickers
- ☐ photocopies of the handout (p. 71)
- ☐ heavy paper or construction paper
- ☐ film or overhead projector or flashlight
- ☐ white cloth
- ☐ objects for the shadow screen
- ☐ bag or box
- ☐ picture of Jesus
- ☐ twisted pretzels
- ☐ apple juice
- ☐ napkins
- ☐ cups

A Look at the Lesson

1. Jesus Is With Me
2. Clothespin Character
3. Crayon Resist
4. Shadow Screen
5. All the Time
6. Listen and Do
7. Follow the Leader
8. Windsock
9. Door Hanger Design
10. Jesus Hugs
11. Picture Pass Around

Young children think in a concrete manner and, therefore, it's difficult for them to understand abstract concepts. They're told that Jesus loves them; however, they can't see him. To help young children understand this abstract concept, we must help them make a connection with concrete activities.

Use this lesson to repeat the theme "Jesus is with me wherever I go." Activities reiterate the theme as well as reinforce the concept.

The Lively Lesson

1. Jesus Is With Me

(You'll need a Bible.)

Gather children in a circle. Lead them in this action song to the tune of "The Mulberry Bush."

This is the way we swing our arms,
Swing our arms, swing our arms.
This is the way we swing our arms,
In praise to the Lord.

Sing other verses and actions such as nod our heads, clap our hands, wiggle our fingers, and march in place.

Once you've gained kids' attention and cooperation, change the song's words. Do the actions in place.

**Jesus is with me when I run,
When I run, when I run.
Jesus is with me when I run,
He's with me wherever I go.**

Sing other verses and actions such as when I walk, jump, skate, stretch, sleep, throw, and eat.

End the activity by singing "Jesus is with me when I sit…" After kids sit, open your Bible to Matthew 28:20b. Tell kids to listen quietly as you read what Jesus said: **"I am with you always."**

Remind kids of the song, and talk briefly about the variety of times Jesus is with them throughout both day and night.

2. Clothespin Character

(You'll need markers and spring clothespins.)
Give each child a spring clothespin and a marker. Let children each draw a face on their clothespin. Show children how to clip their Clothespin Character onto a piece of their clothing.

Say: **Jesus is with us all the time. Every time you look down today and see your Clothespin Character on your clothes, remember that Jesus is with you wherever you go.**

3. Crayon Resist

(You'll need a white crayon and white sheet of construction paper for each child. You'll also need watercolors, paintbrushes, and old shirts or aprons.)
Cover kids' clothes with old shirts or aprons. Give each child a white crayon and a sheet of white construction paper. Instruct kids to draw a scribble design all over the paper, pressing hard with the crayon. Talk with them about how difficult it is to see the design. Then let kids paint over the entire surface of the paper with watercolors. The design will appear on the page as the crayon wax resists the paint. Share with kids that Jesus is also with us even though we can't see him.

4. Shadow Screen

(Gather a variety of objects recognizable by shape, such as a rock, pencil, cup, and fork. Place them in a bag or a box. Add a cut-out shape of Jesus. Then construct a simple shadow screen by placing a thin white cloth in front of a beam of light from a flashlight or slide projector. Nail the cloth to a wooden frame or drape it over a table. If possible, enlist the aid of a helper for this activity.)

Set children in front of the shadow screen. Place one of the objects in the beam of light, behind the cloth. Ask kids to guess what it is by looking at the shadow. Follow this procedure with all of the shapes, and end with the cut-out shape of Jesus. Say: **Just as we knew what all the other shapes were, we also knew Jesus. Jesus is with us even though we can't see him.**

If kids don't recognize Jesus, say: **Even though we didn't recognize Jesus like the other things, he's always with us.**

5. All the Time

Sing this song to the tune of "Did You Ever See a Lassie?" After you've taught the children the words, encourage them to pick a partner to sing the song to.

**Oh, don't you know that Jesus
That Jesus, that Jesus,
Oh, don't you know that Jesus
Is always with you?**

He's with you in daytime.
He's with you at nighttime.
Oh, don't you know that Jesus
Is always with you?

6. Listen and Do

Ask children each to find a place on the floor, kneel down, touch their chin to their chest, and cover their closed eyes with their hands. Tiptoe quietly to a spot and say:
**Peanut butter and strawberry jam,
Can you point to where I am?**

Ask kids to keep their eyes closed and point to you. Tiptoe to a new location and repeat the activity several times. When finished, reinforce that the children knew you were there even though they couldn't see you. Remind kids that we know Jesus is here even though we can't see him.

7. Follow the Leader

Gather children in a circle. Walk around them as you sing the following song to the tune of "The Farmer in the Dell."
**Jesus loves me so.
Yes, Jesus loves me so.
He is with me day and night,
He's there wherever I go.**

As you finish, tap a child on the head and ask him or her to follow you around the circle. Encourage the children to sing with you and continue until everyone is following you.

Keep singing the verse and begin to lead the group around the room. Add an action they can do while singing. For example, tap head, twirl slowly or clap hands above head. At the end of the verse, go to the back of the line and direct the child in front to lead with an action. Continue with the activity until everyone has had an opportunity to lead.

If a child hesitates to lead, invite him or her to come join you, and continue with the next person.

Conclude the activity by gathering in a circle, holding hands, singing the verse, and adding a jump and a "Hey!" at the end.

8. Windsock

(You'll need a 9x12-inch sheet of construction paper, crepe paper, tape, and stickers.)

Say: **Even though we can't see the wind, we can sometimes see that the wind is blowing. Just like we can't see the wind, we can't see Jesus, but we know he's real!**

Take a sheet of 9x12-inch construction paper, and have children tape strips of crepe paper along one of the long sides. Let children decorate the paper with stickers. Bend the paper into a cylinder and tape the ends together. Take the windsock outside, and let the children see the crepe paper blow in the wind, or place it in front of a fan while you talk about how Jesus is always with us even if we can't see him.

If time allows, let each child make a windsock to take home as a reminder that Jesus is real and is with them.

9. Door Hanger Design

(Photocopy the "Door Hanger" handout on page 71, one for each child. Photocopy them onto heavy paper or glue them on construction paper. Provide crayons, small pieces of different colors of tissue paper, and glue.)

Give each child a "Door Hanger" handout. Read the words on it: **Jesus is with me!** Let kids decorate the hangers with crayons or by gluing crumpled tissue paper on them.

Encourage kids to hang their door hangers on a doorknob at home, and to tell their family members that Jesus is with them, too!

10. Jesus Hugs

(You'll need twisted pretzels, apple juice, napkins, and cups.)

Serve pretzels and juice as a snack. Before children eat, have them look at the pretzels and notice the cross pattern. Have them each cross their arms in front of their chest in the same manner. Call this a "Jesus hug." Say that even though we can't see Jesus, we can still feel his love.

With their arms crossed, lead children in this prayer: **Thank you, Jesus, for loving us and being with us wherever we go. Thank you for food to make our bodies strong. Help us to feel your love every day. In Jesus' name, amen.**

11. Picture Pass Around

(You'll need a picture of Jesus.)

Gather in a circle once more. Repeat this adapted verse from Matthew 28:20b: **I am with you always.** Show the children the picture of Jesus, then say: **Pictures of Jesus remind us that he is with us wherever we go.**

Pass the picture around the circle. As each child holds the picture, have him or her complete the sentence: "Jesus is with me when I _____."

Accept each answer even if it's repeated. Suggested answers can be sleep, run, jump, talk, eat, or cry.

When the picture returns to you, sum up all the responses as you lead children in the following reading. Fill in the blank with one of the kids' words, and repeat until all the responses have been included.

Teacher: **For being with us when we ____ _____,**

Children: **Thank you, Jesus!**

Door Hanger

"I am with you always" (Matthew 28:20b).

Jesus is with me!

Permission to copy this handout from *Lively Bible Lessons for MOPPETS* granted for local church use.
Copyright © Group Publishing, Inc., P.O. Box 481, Loveland, CO 80539. www.group.com

Talking to God

A Powerful Purpose
Preschool children will understand what prayer is and that God hears their prayers.

A Sprinkling of Supplies

- [ ] Bible
- [ ] photocopies of the handouts (pp. 76-78)
- [ ] construction paper question mark
- [ ] puppets
- [ ] table
- [ ] basket
- [ ] fish-shaped crackers
- [ ] juice
- [ ] cups
- [ ] napkins
- [ ] paper
- [ ] crayons
- [ ] a pen
- [ ] safety scissors
- [ ] poster board or heavy paper
- [ ] hole punch
- [ ] yarn
- [ ] two plastic cups
- [ ] a long string
- [ ] tissue paper
- [ ] empty baby food jars
- [ ] glue mixed with water
- [ ] paintbrushes

A Look at the Lesson

1. What Is Prayer?
2. Phoning God
3. Are You Listening?
4. God Answers Prayer
5. Fishy Snack
6. Prayer Topics
7. Prayer Bracelets
8. Pray Always
9. God Listens
10. Basket of Prayers
11. Prayer Jar
12. Thank You, God

Many young children love to pray, but they have lots of questions about how prayer works. They need to know that prayer is one way to talk to God. God hears our prayers, and God answers our prayers.

Use this lesson to teach children more about prayer—a way to talk to God.

The Lively Lesson

1. What Is Prayer?

(Use puppets to perform the "What Is Prayer?" skit on page 76. Turn a table on its side to use as a puppet stage. You'll also need a construction paper question mark.)

Welcome the children into the room, and ask them to sit down. Introduce the two puppets, and say: **Let's listen to these two people and see what we're going to learn today.**

When the puppets finish, have the children show their appreciation by giving the puppets a standing ovation. Stand and clap and cheer!

2. Phoning God

(Before class, you'll need to create a "telephone" using a long string tied to two plastic cups.)

Have the children sit in a circle.

Say: **We can talk to God just like we talk to our moms and dads even though we can't see God. That's called prayer. Prayer is kind of like talking to God on the telephone.** Pass one end of the phone to a child in the circle and have him or her hold it up to one ear. Quietly talk into the other end of the phone. Say: **"We can talk to God any time, day or night. God loves you."** Then pass your end to another child, and have the child who was holding the cup share a message with this child. Continue around the circle until everyone in the circle has had a chance to talk into the phone and listen to a message about God's love.

3. Are You Listening?

Say: **Let's sing a song about talking to God, which is called prayer.**

Sing the following song to the tune of "Baa, Baa, Black Sheep." Once children have learned the song, sing the first two lines to them and encourage children to respond back to you with the second two lines.

**Little children
Can you hear?** *(Cup hand to ear.)*
Yes ma'am [sir], yes ma'am [sir] *(nod head)*,
With our ears. *(Cup hand to ear.)*

Pray for your mommy *(fold hands in prayer)*,
Pray for your dad.
And don't forget to pray *(wag finger)*
Even when you're sad. *(Make a sad face.)*

**Little children
Can you hear?** *(Cup hand to ear.)*
Yes ma'am [sir], yes ma'am [sir] *(nod head)*,
With our ears. *(Cup hand to ear.)*

Repeat the song several times.

4. God Answers Prayer

(You'll need a Bible, a basket, and cut-out fish and loaves from photocopies of the "Fish and Loaves" handout on page 77.)

Read aloud about Jesus feeding a crowd of people in Matthew 14:13-21. Then tell children they're going to act out the story.

Ask one of the older children to be Jesus. Give this child a basket with the cut-out fish and loaves in the bottom. You'll need enough fish and loaves to distribute to each child and still have some left over. Don't allow the other children to see in the bottom of the basket.

Choose two or three others to be disciples. Give them five loaves of bread and two fish.

Everyone else plays the hungry crowd.

Narrate the story, and help children act out their parts.

Say: **Jesus saw a huge crowd of people and felt sorry for them.** *("Jesus" looks around at the crowd of people.)*

It was late in the day, and they were hungry. *(Kids rub their tummies and moan, "We're hungry.")*

The disciples came to Jesus. *("Disciples" walk toward Jesus.)*

They said: "We can't feed them. We only have five loaves of bread and two fish." *(Show the five loaves and two fish to Jesus.)*

Jesus said, "Give them to me." *(Disciples give them to Jesus.)*

He took them *(take them)*,
Looked up to heaven *(look up)*,
Prayed over them *(hold up the loaves and fish)*,
Put them in a basket *(put them in your basket)*,
And said, "Give them to the people." *(Jesus says, "Give them to the people.")*

The disciples gave out the food. *(Disciples take Jesus' basket and give out the food to each person in the crowd.)*

The people ate until they were full. *(Pretend to eat the fish and loaves, then lean back and groan, "Oh, we're full.")*

Everyone was amazed because there were 12 baskets of food left over. *(Everyone says, "Wow!")*

After the story, have kids give themselves a standing ovation. Stand and clap and cheer!

Afterward say: **When we pray, God hears our prayers and answers them. We're going to learn more about prayer today.**

5. Fishy Snack

(You'll need fish-shaped crackers, juice, cups, and napkins.)

Tell children they're going to eat some food like the people did in the Bible story. Serve fish-shaped crackers, and distribute cups of juice. Pray before the snack, asking God to bless the food.

6. Prayer Topics

(You'll need photocopies of the "Prayer Topics" handout on page 78 and crayons. Photocopy the handout on poster board or heavy paper.)

When kids finish their snack, give them each a "Prayer Topics" handout and some crayons. Explain the things we pray about shown on the handout: when we get hurt, when we're afraid, our family, someone who is sick, and food.

Say: **Color the pictures. Think about each thing as you color its picture. What else do you pray about? Draw those things in the blank squares. Maybe you have a problem with a friend or you're worried about your parents. God wants us to pray about all of our concerns.**

7. Prayer Bracelets

(You'll need safety scissors, a hole punch, and short pieces of yarn.)

Encourage children each to choose one thing they'd like to pray about today. Help each child cut that picture from the "Prayer Topics" handout.

Assist the children in punching a hole in each square and threading a short piece of yarn through the hole to make a bracelet. Loosely tie the prayer bracelet around the child's wrist. Make a bracelet for yourself, too.

8. Pray Always

Ask kids to gather in a circle. Help them memorize this paraphrase of 1 Thessalonians 5:16-18. You say a phrase and show an action. Then have children repeat what you say and do.

Be happy. *(Smile.)*

Pray always. *(Fold hands, bow heads.)*

Thank God for everything. *(Hold both hands up, look up to heaven.)*

After kids memorize the words and actions, do the actions and ask kids to supply the words.

Finally, have everyone do a silent version of the memorized verse. Have everyone do the actions only—no words.

9. God Listens

(You'll need slips of paper and a pen.)

Have children sit on the floor in front of you. Show them your bracelet, and tell them what you want to pray about. Write your prayer request on a slip of paper.

Tell children they can pray to God and that he always listens. God wants us to tell him any problem or any concern we have. He'll answer our prayers.

One at a time, ask children each to show their bracelets and tell what they want to pray for. Write each child's request on a slip of paper, then hand the slip to the child.

After each child receives his or her slip, all children say, "God listens when we pray" and pat their knees for each syllable.

10. Basket of Prayers

(You'll need the slips of prayer requests and the basket you used in the "God Answers Prayer" activity.)

Tell children: **You're each holding a slip of paper that tells your prayer request. One at a time, stand up, come to me, and put your prayer request in this basket.**

After your basket is full, invite kids to pray silently for the requests. Have kids bow their heads and fold their hands.

Hold up the basket and say: **Dear God, thank you for hearing our prayers. We trust you to answer them. In Jesus' name, amen.**

11. Prayer Jar

(You'll need tissue paper, empty baby food jars, glue mixed with water, and paintbrushes.)

Have children tear tissue paper into small pieces as you say: **We've all mentioned things we want to pray about. We're going to make prayer jars to help us remember that God answers our prayers. Your prayer jar can be a special jar that you put a little rock into every time you see God answer a prayer.**

Give each child a baby food jar and a paintbrush. Show children how to coat the baby food jar with the glue and water mixture. Then let them place pieces of tissue paper over the mixture. Let the baby food jars dry, and then let children take them home.

12. Thank You, God

Remind kids that their memory verse said to pray always and thank God for everything.

One at a time, have kids say one thing they're thankful for. After each child says an item, have all kids clap and shout, "Thank you, God!" Let every person contribute, with the whole group shouting, "Thank you, God!" after each contribution.

What Is Prayer?

Actor 1: *(Claps and jumps all around while looking up.)*

Actor 2: *(Enters.)* Hi. What are you doing?

Actor 1: *(Keeps clapping.)* Shhh.

Actor 2: *(Looks all around, confused. Then looks up.)* Hey, what is it? Why are you clapping?

Actor 1: I'm not clapping.

Actor 2: Oh, yes, you are.

Actor 1: No, I'm not. I'm praying.

Actor 2: That's not praying. When you pray you bow your head and you have to be quiet.

Actor 1: Yeah, I do that sometimes. But right now I'm just telling God how great I think he is. Why don't you join me? Yea, God!

Actor 2: *(Joins, and both say, "Yea, God!" and clap.)*

Actor 2: *(Bends over and picks up a question mark.)* Wait a minute. Wait a minute.

Actor 1: Now what?

Actor 2: I want to ask God a question. Is that OK?

Actor 1: Sure it is. That's part of prayer, too.

Actor 2: You mean if we don't understand something, we can ask God about it in prayer?

Actor 1: Sure! God wants us to ask questions. So go ahead.

Actor 2: *(Bows head, then looks up.)* OK, I'm doing it.

Actor 1: Well, what'd you ask?

Actor 2: I asked God to teach me more about prayer because I like talking to him.

Permission to copy this handout from *Lively Bible Lessons for MOPPETS* granted for local church use.
Copyright © Group Publishing, Inc., P.O. Box 481, Loveland, CO 80539. www.group.com

Fish and Loaves

Permission to copy this handout from *Lively Bible Lessons for MOPPETS* granted for local church use.
Copyright © Group Publishing, Inc., P.O. Box 481, Loveland, CO 80539. www.group.com

Prayer Topics

Be happy. Pray always. Thank God for everything
(adapted from 1 Thessalonians 5:16-18).

Be happy. Pray always. Thank God for everything
(adapted from 1 Thessalonians 5:16-18).

Be happy. Pray always. Thank God for everything
(adapted from 1 Thessalonians 5:16-18).

Be happy. Pray always. Thank God for everything
(adapted from 1 Thessalonians 5:16-18).

Be happy. Pray always. Thank God for everything
(adapted from 1 Thessalonians 5:16-18).

Be happy. Pray always. Thank God for everything
(adapted from 1 Thessalonians 5:16-18).

Be happy. Pray always. Thank God for everything
(adapted from 1 Thessalonians 5:16-18).

Be happy. Pray always. Thank God for everything
(adapted from 1 Thessalonians 5:16-18).

Permission to copy this handout from *Lively Bible Lessons for MOPPETS* granted for local church use.
Copyright © Group Publishing, Inc., P.O. Box 481, Loveland, CO 80539. www.group.com

God's Gift—Forgiveness

A Powerful Purpose
Preschool children will learn that Jesus forgives us and wants us to forgive others.

A Sprinkling of Supplies

- [ ] Bible
- [ ] masking tape
- [ ] paper
- [ ] marker
- [ ] colorful stickers
- [ ] paper plates
- [ ] napkins
- [ ] cups
- [ ] juice
- [ ] cheese and crackers
- [ ] photocopies of the handout (p. 83)
- [ ] crayons
- [ ] chairs
- [ ] CD of lively music
- [ ] CD player
- [ ] pudding
- [ ] paper plates
- [ ] wet wipes
- [ ] vinyl tablecloth

A Look at the Lesson

1. Which Way Do I Go?
2. A Bible Story
3. Forgive All of Our Friends
4. Banquet Time
5. We Are All Forgiven
6. How Do You Feel?
7. Forgive Others
8. Memory Tune
9. Musical Chairs
10. Forgiveness Prayer

We all feel guilty at times *and are hard on ourselves. We wish we would've done things differently. We kick ourselves for saying something mean or selfish.*

Preschoolers are not immune to guilt. They may feel sorry when they do something wrong, hurt their brothers or sisters, or hit their friends. Some innocent children feel guilty when their parents divorce.

Use this lesson to talk about the forgiveness Jesus offers.

The Lively Lesson

1. Which Way Do I Go?

(Use masking tape to lay out two different "roads" as shown in the diagram. Begin at your room's entrance and end up on the other side. Put a happy face on the wall at the end of one road and a sad face at the end of the other road. You'll also need colorful stickers.)

Greet each child, and tell him or her to choose one of the roads and follow it to the end. Say: **If you find a happy face at the end of your road, sit down below the sign. If you find a sad face, go back and follow the other road.**

When everyone is sitting under the happy face, give kids each a colorful sticker. Say: **Sometimes we do bad things. That's like going down the wrong road. But if we do something bad, God will forgive us if we ask him to. Then we can continue on a good road by doing what's right. God's forgiveness makes us happy.**

2. A Bible Story

(You'll need a Bible.)

Say: **Here's a Bible story about a son who took the wrong road and did the wrong thing. When the son felt bad for what he did, he told his father, "I'm sorry." His dad said: "It's OK. I love you." His dad forgave him.**

Read from a children's Bible the story of the prodigal son in Luke 15:11-24.

Say: **God is like the father in the story who forgave his son. When the son admitted he'd sinned, the father forgave him. God always forgives us when we ask for his forgiveness, and he wants us to forgive others who do bad things to us.**

Have children stand. Tell kids you're going to read some questions. If their answer is "happy," they should jump up and down and say "happy." If their answer is "sad," they should slowly sit down and say "sad."

Practice a couple of times. Then read these questions:

• **At the end of the story, how do you think the dad felt when his boy returned home?**

• **At the beginning of the story, how do you think the dad felt about his son leaving?**

• **How do you think the younger son felt when he returned home and his dad welcomed him and forgave him?**

• **How do you feel when someone forgives you and says, "It's OK"?**

3. Forgive All of Our Friends

Sing the following song to the tune of "The Old Gray Mare."

Jesus wants us *(point up)*
To forgive all of our friends *(hug a friend),*
Forgive all of our friends *(hug a friend),*
Forgive all of our friends. *(Hug a friend.)*
Jesus wants us *(point up)*
To forgive all of our friends *(hug a friend)*
Because he forgives us. *(Hug yourself.)*

Because he forgives us *(hug yourself),*
Because he forgives us. *(Hug yourself.)*
Jesus wants us *(point up)*
To forgive all of our friends *(hug a friend)*
Because he forgives us. *(Hug yourself.)*

4. Banquet Time

(Prepare a table with paper plates, napkins, cups, juice, cheese, and crackers.)

Ask:

• **How would you feel if I said that we're going to eat snacks and celebrate God's forgiveness?**

Tell kids that they look like they would enjoy a forgiveness banquet—like the man gave his son in the story. Lead them to the table, and sit down for a meal. Distribute paper plates, napkins, and cups.

Pass around the cheese and crackers and say: **Eat some cheese and crackers. Fill up. God blesses us so much we overflow with his goodness.**

Fill each cup with juice and say: **Drink this juice and remember that all good things—especially forgiveness—come from God.**

5. We Are All Forgiven

Play a post-banquet party game. Teach kids these words to the tune of "Ten Little Indians."

**God forgives his little children.
God forgives his little children.
God forgives his little children
When they say, "I'm sorry."**

Gather in a circle, and sing the song as you march clockwise. The second time you sing, have kids each find a partner, face each other, grab hands, and go sideways around the circle counterclockwise. The third time you sing, have everyone march clockwise again.

6. How Do You Feel?

(You'll need photocopies of the "How Do You Feel?" handout on page 83 and crayons.)

Sit down in the circle after you finish the song. Give kids each a "How Do You Feel?" handout and crayons. Tell them to hold the handout so the face looks happy. Next, have them turn the handout upside down. The face now looks sad. Give children a couple of minutes to color the face.

Say: **I'm going to ask you a few questions. If the answer is "happy," hold up the happy face. If the answer is "sad," turn the paper so the sad face shows.**

Ask:
- **How do you feel after our banquet?**
- **How do you feel when someone hurts you?**
- **How do you feel when you forgive that person and say, "It's OK"?**
- **How would you feel if I said, "It's time to say goodbye"?**
- **How would you feel if I said, "We still have more fun activities to do, we won't say goodbye for a while"?**

7. Forgive Others

(Each child will need the "How Do You Feel?" handout.)

Say: **When God forgives us, we feel good. Others feel good when we forgive them. I'll read some stories, and you answer my questions by turning your paper to a smile or a frown, depending on your answer.**

- **Tiffany was playing with Tom's toy lawnmower and broke off one of its wheels. How does Tiffany feel? How does Tom feel?**
- **Tom got angry at Tiffany and made her go away. How does Tiffany feel? How does Tom feel?**
- **Tom said he would forgive Tiffany and gave Tiffany another toy to play with. How does Tiffany feel? How does Tom feel? How does God feel?**
- **Jeff, Chris, and Terry are playing together in the yard. How do they feel?**
- **Jeff and Chris ignore Terry and won't let her play with them. How does Terry feel?**
- **Terry gets mad and starts yelling. How does Terry feel?**
- **Jeff and Chris say they're sorry, and Terry forgives them. They keep playing. How does Terry feel? How does God feel? How do Jeff and Chris feel?**

8. Memory Tune

(You'll need a CD of lively music and a CD player.)

Let kids learn this Bible verse in a fun way: Forgive each other (adapted from Ephesians 4:32). Play lively music, and ask kids to move around the room—hop, skip, walk, march, any movement they want. When you stop the music, have children each hug a person standing close to them and say, "Forgive each other." Start the music again, and continue until kids have each hugged several different people and repeated the verse several times.

9. Musical Chairs

(You'll need chairs set up in a circle, enough for every child.)

Play a game of Musical Chairs, only don't eliminate anyone. Have children march around the chairs and sing the following song with you. When you stop singing, they should all sit down. Choose a child to begin the song to start kids marching again. Sing the song to the tune of "Row, Row, Row Your Boat."

Say you're sorry,
Sorry when you're wrong.
God forgives us
When we say
We're sorry when we're wrong.

10. Forgiveness Prayer

(You'll need pudding, paper plates, a vinyl tablecloth, and wet wipes.)

Give each child a mound of pudding on a paper plate. Allow children to draw shapes in the pudding as they think about God's forgiveness. Encourage children to think of one thing they've done wrong. Have them draw a frown in their pudding to show that God is sad when we do wrong.

Explain that children will each say: **God, thank you for forgiving me for** [what they thought of]. Then they'll smooth the pudding to erase the frowns they drew, just as God erases our sins when he forgives us. Let kids draw smiles to show that God loves us and wants to forgive us. Close by thanking God for sending Jesus to die for our sins. Then say: **In Jesus' name, amen.**

How Do You Feel?

Forgive each other
(adapted from Ephesians 4:32).

Permission to copy this handout from *Lively Bible Lessons for MOPPETS* granted for local church use.
Copyright © Group Publishing, Inc., P.O. Box 481, Loveland, CO 80539. www.group.com

Heaven: Home, Sweet Home

A Powerful Purpose
Preschool children will learn that heaven is a place they'll like.

A Look at the Lesson

1. Squirrel at Home
2. Heavenly Song
3. In a Sack
4. Seeing Is Believing
5. Pictures of Home
6. What Makes a Home?
7. Heaven: Home, Sweet Home
8. What Is Heaven?
9. Treasure in Heaven Craft
10. Someday in Heaven
11. Heavenly Honey Biscuits

A Sprinkling of Supplies

- [ ] Bible
- [ ] doll in a sack
- [ ] large pieces of construction paper
- [ ] crayons
- [ ] photocopies of the handout (p. 88)
- [ ] 1 empty plastic soda bottle with lid per child
- [ ] craft sand
- [ ] uniquely shaped beads
- [ ] small funnel
- [ ] modeling dough
- [ ] biscuits
- [ ] butter
- [ ] honey in squeeze bottles
- [ ] juice
- [ ] cups
- [ ] napkins
- [ ] supplies to clean hands

It is hard for a child to get a clear and reassuring picture of our eternal home. Simplify this concept by comparing heaven to the very best earthly home.

Use this lesson to show kids that though we don't know everything about heaven, we do know one important fact: Heaven will one day be our home, where we'll live with our heavenly Father and the wonderful family he has given us to love.

The Lively Lesson

1. Squirrel at Home

Welcome the children, and play a fun game to get them ready to learn. Have kids form teams of three. Have two members of each team make a "hollow tree" by standing facing each other, with their hands on each other's shoulders. Have the third team member play a "squirrel" by standing between the other two, at home in the tree. When you clap your hands, each squirrel must find a new home tree.

Play a few times, then switch so the "hollow trees" can be squirrels, too. Rotate in any players who didn't get to play the first round.

Say: **You all played squirrels at home in their trees. Our homes are in houses or apartments. But today we're going to talk about heaven—our home when we go to live with Jesus forever.**

2. Heavenly Song

Say: **Let's sing a song about heaven, where God and Jesus live.** Sing this song to the tune of "Mary Had a Little Lamb." Encourage children to clap along to the song with you as they learn the words.

**Heaven is a special place,
Special place, special place.
Heaven is a special place,
And heaven is our home.**

**Jesus lives in heaven now,
Heaven now, heaven now.
Jesus lives in heaven now,
And heaven is our home.**

**We can live there, too, with God,
There with God, there with God.
We can live there, too, with God.
Yes, heaven is our home.**

3. In a Sack

(You'll need a doll in a sack.)
Hold up the sack with the doll inside. Ask the children to describe the doll you're holding up. They may be able to guess that it has arms and legs and a face, but since they can't see it, they won't be able to describe it in detail.

Take the doll out of the bag. Hold it up so everyone can see it, then say: **Now tell me what the doll looks like.** They'll tell you all they can see: hair color, eye color, what it's wearing.

4. Seeing Is Believing

Pass around the doll while you discuss these questions:
• **Why couldn't you describe the doll when it was in a sack?**
• **Were there things you could guess about the doll even when you couldn't see it?**

Say: **It's hard to describe something you can't see. That's just like heaven. It's hard to describe because we haven't seen it yet.**

5. Pictures of Home

(You'll need crayons and large pieces of construction paper. Lay them on the floor.)
Have kids follow you to the construction paper and crayons. As they follow you, march to the chant:

**Heaven is a wonderful place;
It will be our home someday.**

Have children each find a piece of paper to draw on. Tell them to draw a picture of their homes. When everyone has finished, lead children on a walking tour around the pictures. As you walk and look, say the chant again.

6. What Makes a Home?

Let each child discuss his or her picture.
Adapt the following discussion depending on the children in your group. Be sensitive to kids whose homes might not be happy—through death or divorce or other reasons. Emphasize that heaven will be better than even the best earthly home.

Say: **Our homes are special places. Most of us like our homes very much, and we** wouldn't feel at home in any other house. Why is that? Is it because of the walls? the rooms? the windows? the furniture? All of our homes probably have these things. So there's nothing really special about them, is there? What does your home have that no other home has?

Let kids try to guess, then say: **The people who live in our homes make our homes special!**

7. Heaven: Home, Sweet Home

(You'll need crayons and photocopies of the "Heaven: Home, Sweet Home" handout on page 88. Lay the handouts and crayons on the floor.)

Ask kids to follow behind you to another area of the room where you've laid the handouts and crayons. As they follow, march to the same chant:

**Heaven is a wonderful place;
It will be our home someday.**

Read the handouts to the kids: "Heaven: Home, Sweet Home." Explain that heaven is a wonderful place to live with God. Say that in heaven, everyone's happy because they're with God. Have kids draw a picture of heaven as they imagine it—pretty clouds, warm sunshine, happy people.

After they finish, walk around their drawings as you say the chant again.

8. What Is Heaven?

(You'll need a Bible.)

Say: **Heaven is God's home. Jesus lives there, and someday we will, too. Listen as I read what Jesus says.**

Read John 14:3: **"When everything is ready, I will come and get you, so that you will always be with me where I am."**

You drew your ideas of heaven. Lots of people wonder what heaven will look like. We haven't seen it yet. Remember how you couldn't describe the doll because you couldn't see it? Well, heaven is hard to describe, too. But the Bible tells us about heaven.

Read the following descriptions, and direct kids to respond after each description.

• **Matthew 6:20 says we will have treasures in heaven.** *(Have kids say, "O-o-o-o-o-o-o.")*

• **John 14:2 says there are many rooms there for lots of people.** *(Have kids spread their arms wide.)*

• **Revelation 19:1 says that those who live in heaven will shout praises to God.** *(Have everyone shout, "I love you, God!")*

• **Revelation 21:3-4 says God will live with us there and will wipe all our tears away. There won't be any more crying or death or sadness.** *(Have everyone smile big smiles.)*

So heaven will one day be the home where God lives with all of us, his children. *(Have everyone link arms in a circle and sit down.)*

9. Treasure in Heaven Craft

(You'll need empty plastic soda bottles with lids, craft sand, small funnel, and uniquely shaped beads.)

Before class, wash the soda bottles and let them dry.

Say: **Matthew 6:20 says we will have treasures in heaven. Let's make a treasure chest to remind us that someday we will live in heaven with God forever.**

Give each child a bottle, and help him or her use a funnel to pour several handfuls of sand into the bottle. Allow children to each pick 7 to 10 of their favorite beads and drop them in their bottles as well. Close the bottles tightly, and let children shake them. Encourage children to search for treasures by rotating the bottle around. Let children take the bottle home to share with their families what they learned about heaven.

10. Someday in Heaven

(You'll need modeling dough.)

Say: **Now that you've heard what the Bible says about heaven, what do you think heaven is like?**

Let children use the modeling dough to create shapes to represent what they imagine heaven will be like. Encourage them to show their creations to their friends and talk about why they're excited about heaven.

11. Heavenly Honey Biscuits

(You'll need biscuits, butter, honey in squeeze bottles, juice, cups, napkins, and supplies to clean hands.)

Serve biscuits with butter and honey, and pour juice into cups. Explain that you're having a sweet snack because heaven will be such a sweet place to live. Then pray: **Thank you, God, that you're making a wonderful home for us in heaven. Thank you for loving us so much that you want to live there with us forever. In Jesus' name, amen.**

Sing songs such as "Heaven Is a Wonderful Place" and "Do, Lord."

Let kids take home their two drawings—their earthly home and their heavenly home—plus their modeling dough creations.

Heaven:
Home, Sweet Home

"When everything is ready, I will come and get you, so that you will always be with me where I am" (John 14:3).

PART 4:

A Lively Look at Celebrations

A Birthday Bonanza

A Powerful Purpose
Preschool children will celebrate their birthdays and see that the bigger they grow, the more they know.

A Look at the Lesson

1. Babies Can't Do This
2. My Handprints: I Am Growing
3. Measuring Growth
4. Picture Growth
5. Birthday Balloons: Getting Bigger and Bigger
6. Happy Birthday to Me
7. Birthday Party Snack
8. Jesus Grew, Too
9. Jesus Was a Child
10. I'm Not a Baby, I'm Not a Grown-Up
11. See How Tall I Grow to Be
12. Thanks for Birthdays and Growing

A Sprinkling of Supplies

- [ ] Bible
- [ ] baby-size doll
- [ ] bright color of tempera paint
- [ ] flat pans
- [ ] old shirts or aprons
- [ ] photocopies of the handout (p. 95)
- [ ] measuring tape
- [ ] craft sticks
- [ ] glitter paint
- [ ] paintbrushes
- [ ] Polaroid camera
- [ ] glue
- [ ] balloons
- [ ] frosted cupcakes
- [ ] napkins
- [ ] items of baby or adult clothing

Preschool children are learning about themselves, especially about what they can do. They're in a concrete stage of learning and don't understand symbolism. Each new learning experience (especially when presented in an active, fun way) provides important information about their capabilities and enhances self-esteem.

Use this lesson to show kids how much they're growing and how they're learning new things.

The Lively Lesson

1. Babies Can't Do This

As children arrive, seat them in a circle. Ask them, one by one:

• **What can you do that a baby can't do? Show me!**
For example, they can run, jump, talk, hop, or sing.

After each child shows you something, say: **When you were a baby, you couldn't do these things. Now you can because you're growing.**

2. My Handprints: I Am Growing

(You'll need the baby-size doll, bright color of tempera paint in flat pans, photocopies of the "My Handprints" handout from page 95, and old shirts or smocks. Ask someone to help you with this activity.)

Pass around the doll, and ask the children each to hold their hand up to the doll's hand. Say: **Something else that tells us we're growing is that we get bigger. Look at your hands and see how much bigger they are than the doll's hands. Are your hands bigger than a baby's hands?**

Tell them they're going to make prints of their hands, which are bigger than a baby's but still smaller than a grown-up's.

Hold up a "My Handprints" handout and read the poem.

**Here are handprints of me,
Made for people to see.
Though to you I seem small,
God will help me grow tall!**

Cover the kids' clothes with the old shirts or smocks. Dip the palm sides of their hands in the tempera paint, and press them firmly on their handouts. Have someone help the children wash their hands afterward. Write each child's name on his or her paper.

3. Measuring Growth

(You'll need a measuring tape.)

Help children understand that they're growing and changing. Use a measuring tape to measure body parts such as hands, arms, or legs. After you measure a body part, hold up the measuring tape for everyone to see.

Say: **See how** [name of child] **is growing.** Turn to the child and affirm him or her by saying: **You're growing every day. God is helping you grow!**

Continue until you've had a chance to measure and affirm each child.

4. Picture Growth

(You'll need craft sticks, glue, glitter paint, paintbrushes, and a Polaroid camera.)

Take a picture of each child with the Polaroid camera. Have each child paint four craft sticks with glitter paint. While the craft sticks are drying, ask children to talk about the things they're learning and how they're growing.

TEACHER TIP

If a Polaroid camera isn't available, use a regular camera to take a picture of each child. Develop the pictures during the week, and let kids assemble their pictures and frames next week. Or use a digital camera and print them on the spot!

When the craft sticks are dry, help children glue the corners of the craft sticks together to form a square or a rectangle to fit the picture. Then turn the frame over and glue the picture onto all sides of the frame.

Encourage children to take their pictures home to remind them that they're growing each day.

5. Birthday Balloons: Getting Bigger and Bigger

(You'll need an inflated balloon for each person. Be aware that some children have allergies to latex balloons. Use non-latex balloons wherever possible. Also, be familiar enough with your children and parents to know of existing allergies.)

Say: **We use balloons to celebrate birthdays. But did you know that a balloon can grow like your body grows?**

Show kids a deflated balloon, then say: **See how small this balloon is? Watch what happens to it.**

Blow into the balloon until it's one-fourth full. Say: **This balloon is like a 1-year-old.** Add a bit more air and say: **Now it's like a 2-year-old.** And so on, until the balloon is "like a 5-year-old." **This balloon grew just as you are growing. I'm going to give you each a balloon. We're going to bat the balloons in the air.**

Give one inflated balloon to each child, and allow a couple of minutes of "balloon-batting." The goal is that the balloons stay in the air. As kids bat balloons, lead them in saying "Growing, growing, we are growing."

After balloons have been batted for a while, gather them. If any balloon breaks, immediately pick up all of the pieces.

6. Happy Birthday to Me

Gather kids in a circle around you. Say: **One thing that happens when we grow is that we have birthdays!** Announce that you're going to celebrate everyone's birthday today and need help singing "Happy Birthday to You" in a new way. Have them sing:

**Happy birthday to me,
Happy birthday to me,
Happy birthday, dear** [all children shout out their own name],
Happy birthday to me!

If you have time, you could sing through the song once for every child.

7. Birthday Party Snack

(You'll need one frosted cupcake for each child and napkins.)

Pass out the frosted cupcakes as you say: Happy birthday, birthday kids. Have some birthday cake.

8. Jesus Grew, Too

(You'll need a Bible.)

While kids are eating, say: **Did you know that Jesus was once a child, too? We celebrate his birthday at Christmas. After Jesus was a baby, he grew to be your age. Listen to what the Bible tells us.**

Read Luke 2:52 from a children's Bible, or use this wording: **"Jesus continued to learn more and more and to grow physically. People liked him, and he pleased God."**

Jesus grew up as a child just like you're growing up.

After kids swallow the last of their cupcakes, say: **Let's sing Jesus a birthday song, too.** Sing these words:

**Happy birthday to you,
Happy birthday to you,
Happy birthday, dear Jesus,
We sure do love you!**

9. Jesus Was a Child

Sing the following song to the tune of "The Wheels on the Bus Go Round and Round." Have children start out crouching down. As you sing, each time you say the word "grew" or "grow," encourage children to stand up a little taller so that by the end of the song, they're standing on tiptoes.

**Jesus was a child who grew and grew,
Grew and grew, grew and grew.
Jesus was a child who grew and grew,
Just like we do.
The friends in our class will grow and grow,
Grow and grow, grow and grow.
The friends in our class will grow and grow,
Just like Jesus grew.**

10. I'm Not a Baby, I'm Not a Grown-Up

(You'll need items of adult and baby clothing, one piece per child.)

Place the baby and adult clothes in the center of the room. Gather children in a circle around the clothes. One at a time, have each child pick out one item of clothing and take it back to his or her seat.

After everyone has done this, go around the circle and invite kids to try on their chosen items. Ask children questions such as:

• **What's wrong with that item? How does it feel? Is it too big or too small?**

With each item of baby clothing, say something like: **Those baby clothes are too small for you.** With each item of adult clothing say something like: **Those grown-up clothes are too big for you.**

After everyone has had a turn, say: **As you can see, you're no longer babies, but you're not yet grown-ups. You are you. Each of you is a special person. You're growing bigger each day, and you'll keep growing. Each inch you grow, each day of your life, you learn new things. That's the way God made you.**

11. See How Tall I Grow to Be

Sing this action song to the tune of "Twinkle, Twinkle, Little Star." Have children repeat each line with actions, then slowly combine all lines together.

See how tall I grow to be. *(Stretch hands above head.)*
Inch by inch I grow, you see. *(Stretch hands above head "inch by inch" with each word.)*
I'm not a baby anymore. *(Rock baby.)*
I'm getting bigger, that's for sure. *(Jump.)*
See how tall I grow to be. *(Stretch on toes.)*
God made you *(point to others),*
And God made me. *(Point to self.)*

12. Thanks for Birthdays and Growing

Ask children to hold hands in a circle and bow their heads. Pray: **Thank you, God, for making me and for giving me a family that loves me. Thank you for each birthday and that I am growing each day. In Jesus' name, amen.**

Give kids their balloons to take home. As you hand out the balloons, say: **Happy Birthday!**

My Handprints

Here are handprints of me,
Made for people to see.
Though to you I seem small,
God will help me grow tall!

Jesus continued to learn more and more and to grow physically. People liked him, and he pleased God (adapted from Luke 2:52).

Permission to copy this handout from *Lively Bible Lessons for MOPPETS* granted for local church use.
Copyright © Group Publishing, Inc., P.O. Box 481, Loveland, CO 80539. www.group.com

The Reason for Easter

A Powerful Purpose
Preschool children will learn more about Jesus and about Easter.

A Look at the Lesson
1. Class Crier
2. Jesus Died for My Sins
3. Resurrection Buns
4. The Easter Story
5. Rock Reminder
6. Eyewitness Report
7. Up, Up, Up
8. Easter Baskets
9. Easter Cross Hunt
10. Eggshell Cross
11. Jesus Rose Again
12. Prayer Time

A Sprinkling of Supplies

- [ ] Bible or a book for children that tells the Easter story
- [ ] three construction paper crosses per child
- [ ] robe for the class crier
- [ ] two Resurrection Buns per child (see recipe on p. 101)
- [ ] sandwich bags
- [ ] photocopies of the handouts (pp. 100-101)
- [ ] three puppets made from socks or sacks
- [ ] cardboard
- [ ] marker
- [ ] tape
- [ ] stapler and staples
- [ ] table
- [ ] Easter stickers
- [ ] scissors
- [ ] one plastic gallon milk jug per child
- [ ] 1 rock per child
- [ ] eggshells
- [ ] glue
- [ ] paper
- [ ] paintbrushes
- [ ] watercolor paints

Easter can mean a lot of things to young children: Easter egg hunts, baskets, and bunnies. Easter can also mean a time of big meals, family gatherings, church services, and songs.
Use this lesson to help children talk about Easter. Help them focus on the real reason for Easter—Jesus.

The Lively Lesson

1. Class Crier

(Ask an adult or teenager to wear a robe and perform as the class crier four times during the lesson. Read the lesson ahead of time to see when the class crier walks through. The person should dress like a follower of Jesus.)

When children have arrived, have the class crier give the first cry: "Oh, my. Jesus is dead. He died on a cross."

Welcome the kids and say: **That was our class crier, who'll tell us Easter messages throughout our time together.**

For Extra Impact

For extra impact during the lesson, use the popular Resurrection Eggs devotion with children. The Resurrection Eggs are available at www.familylife.com.
Warning: Contains Small Parts: Not recommended for children under 3 years

2. Jesus Died for My Sins

Ask kids to join hands in a circle and walk clockwise as they sing this song to the tune of "London Bridge."

**Jesus died for my sins,
For my sins,
For my sins.
Jesus died for my sins;
I'm forgiven.**

Have kids sing the song several times, then sit down in a circle. Say: **We're going to talk about Easter—about Jesus dying for our sins and rising from the dead. When Jesus died on a cross, he was buried in a tomb, which is a cave for people who have died.**

Have the class crier cry a second time: "Oh, no. Jesus is buried in a tomb."

Say: **But that's not the end of the story.**

3. Resurrection Buns

(You'll need Resurrection Buns made according to the recipe on the handout on page 101.)

Give each child a Resurrection Bun. As kids bite into their buns, they'll discover the buns' hollow insides contain a sugary surprise.

Say: **You're surprised at the inside of your Resurrection Bun. The disciples were also surprised on the first Easter. They went inside the tomb where Jesus was buried and discovered something. It was empty.**

Have the class crier give the third cry: "I'm so sad that Jesus is dead."

4. The Easter Story

(You'll need a children's Bible or a book that tells the Easter story for children.)

Read the Easter story from John 20:1-8 or from a children's book.

Ask kids to close their eyes and picture the story in their minds. Imagine…
- early morning,
- going to the tomb,
- seeing the big rock used to cover the opening was rolled away,
- Mary running to tell the others,
- Peter and the other disciple running back to the tomb,
- seeing the tomb was empty,
- Jesus was not there.

Have the class crier cry out the fourth time: "He's alive! He's alive! He's alive!"

5. Rock Reminder

(You'll need paint, paintbrushes, and rocks.)

Take children on a walk outside to pick rocks, or have a selection of rocks already in the room. Allow children to each pick a favorite rock. Then let them paint the rocks.

Say: **Jesus died on the cross, was buried, but then rose from the dead. When the disciples went to visit the tomb, the big rock covering the front of the tomb had been rolled away. The tomb was empty because Jesus is alive!**

Let the paint dry, and have kids take their rocks home to remind them of the empty tomb and why we celebrate Easter.

6. Eyewitness Report

(You'll need the "Eyewitness Report" skit on page 100 and three puppets—a reporter and two disciples. Make simple puppets out of socks or sacks. Use a marker to design faces. Tape a cardboard microphone to the front of the

reporter puppet. Ask three adults or teenagers to perform this puppet skit. Turn a table on its side and use it for a stage.)

Have everyone follow the class crier around the room. Everyone should march behind the crier chanting, "He's alive! He's alive! He's alive!" The class crier should lead kids to the puppet stage.

When kids are seated, begin the Eyewitness Report puppet show.

7. Up, Up, Up

After the puppet show, say: **We're going to celebrate that surprising report that Jesus is alive and rose from the dead.**

Teach children this Easter action song to the tune of "Row, Row, Row Your Boat." Repeat the song and actions several times.

Up (touch the floor),
Up (touch your thighs),
Up (touch your shoulders)
He rose (wave hands above head);
Jesus is alive. (Clap, clap, clap.)
Jesus is alive today. (Wave hands above head.)
Jesus is alive. (Clap, clap, clap.)

8. Easter Baskets

(For each child, you'll need an empty plastic gallon milk jug. You'll also need scissors, a stapler, and Easter stickers. Cut the gallon jugs in half. Cut a 1-inch ring from the bottom of the upper half of the jug. Clip the ring to make a strip of plastic. Staple this strip to the bottom half of the jug to make a handle for the basket as shown in the diagram.)

Say: **Let's make Easter baskets. Decorate them any way you want.**

Let children use the stickers to decorate their baskets. You make one, too, so kids can see an example.

9. Easter Cross Hunt

(For each child, you'll need three construction paper crosses.)

While kids finish decorating their baskets, hide the crosses in the room.

Say: **Since Jesus is the real reason for Easter, we're not going to look for Easter eggs today; we're going to look for Easter crosses. We're celebrating because Jesus died on a cross and lives again.**

Let kids hunt for the Easter crosses and put them in their baskets. Then let kids take turns hiding the crosses and letting others hunt for them. After your game, divide the crosses evenly among the children.

10. Eggshell Cross

(You'll need eggshells, glue, paper, paintbrushes, and watercolor paints.)

Collect eggshells and crush them into small pieces.

Say: **Let's make our own crosses to remind us why we celebrate Easter.**

Show children how to glue the eggshells onto a piece of paper in the shape of a cross. When the glue dries, have children paint over the shells with watercolors.

Make sure to have children wash their hands after touching the eggshells.

11. Jesus Rose Again

When children have finished making their crosses, sing "Jesus Rose Again" to the tune of "Oh, Be Careful Little Eyes."

Oh, Jesus died on the cross for us all. (Form fingers in the shape of a cross.)

Oh, Jesus dies on the cross for us all. *(Form fingers in the shape of a cross.)*

God gave up his Son, Jesus, because God so-o loved us. *(Cross arms over chest.)*

Oh, Jesus died on the cross for us all. *(Form fingers in the shape of a cross.)*

Jesus rose from the grave to live again. *(Jump up and spread arms wide.)*

Jesus rose from the grave to live again. *(Jump up and spread arms wide.)*

Jesus took away our sin, so now we can live with him. *(Make a throwing motion.)*

Jesus rose from the grave to live again. *(Jump up and spread arms wide.)*

12. Prayer Time

(For each child, you'll need a photocopy of the "Resurrection Buns" handout on page 98 and a Resurrection Bun in a sandwich bag.)

Gather the children. Instead of forming a circle, form a cross. Pray: **Thank you, Jesus, for dying for us on the cross and for rising from the dead on Easter. In Jesus' name, amen.**

Give kids each a photocopy of the "Resurrection Buns" handout, and put a wrapped Resurrection Bun in each child's basket. Let kids take their baskets home and have a wonderful Easter.

Eyewitness Report

The Reporter puppet stands on the stage. Two Disciple puppets run across the stage and almost knock the Reporter over.

Reporter: Hey, what's going on here?

Disciple 1: Haven't you heard the news?

Disciple 2: I thought everyone knew by now!

Reporter: What news? Knew what? *(Points microphone toward each puppet's face as he talks.)*

Disciple 1: He's alive!

Disciple 2: He has risen!

Reporter: What? Are you saying a dead person is now alive?

Both: Yes! Jesus is alive! *(Reporter is confused about where to point the microphone.)*

Reporter: Jesus? Who is this Jesus?

Disciple 1: He is the Son of God.

Reporter: And you say he died. How did this Jesus die?

Disciple 2: It was three days ago. The saddest day of our lives.

Disciple 1: They hung Jesus on a cross and killed him.

Reporter: What did he do wrong?

Disciple 1: Nothing. They just wanted to kill him.

Disciple 2: And he died. And we thought it was all over.

Disciple 1: But today we saw him! We saw his hands and feet where the nails had been.

Disciple 2: And he ate with us.

Reporter: A dead man is alive? How?

Disciple 1: God raised him from the dead.

Reporter: Why did God raise Jesus from the dead?

Disciple 2: So we can live forever, just like Jesus!

Reporter: What?

Disciple 1: Don't you see? Jesus is God's gift to us. If we accept God's gift of Jesus, we'll live forever, too.

Reporter: *(Turns to audience.)* Well, you heard it, folks. Jesus was killed and buried in a tomb for three days. But now he's alive. This is Perry Puppet reporting live from Jerusalem on Easter morning.

Permission to copy this handout from *Lively Bible Lessons for MOPPETS* granted for local church use.
Copyright © Group Publishing, Inc., P.O. Box 481, Loveland, CO 80539. www.group.com

Resurrection Buns

Frozen bread dough
Butter
24 marshmallows
1 cup sugar
2 teaspoons cinnamon

Let the frozen dough thaw.
Melt some butter.
In a separate bowl, mix the sugar and cinnamon together.
Divide dough into 24 uniform balls. Roll each ball out until flat. Wrap each flattened ball around a marshmallow, making sure to seal all openings. Dip the ball in melted butter, then in the sugar and cinnamon mixture.
Place in a large, greased baking pan. Cover and let rise until double (about 35 minutes). Bake at 375 degrees for 18 to 20 minutes. Makes 24.

"He is risen from the dead"
(Luke 24:6b).

A Thankful Thanksgiving

A Sprinkling of Supplies

- ☐ Bible
- ☐ sidewalk chalk
- ☐ one pint of cold heavy whipping cream
- ☐ one see-through plastic container with a tight-fitting lid
- ☐ crackers
- ☐ knife
- ☐ a small bowl
- ☐ chocolate milk
- ☐ cups
- ☐ napkins
- ☐ different types of seeds (pumpkin, sunflower, sesame, apple)
- ☐ different colors of construction paper
- ☐ glue
- ☐ tape measure
- ☐ butcher paper
- ☐ scissors
- ☐ marker
- ☐ crayons
- ☐ bulletin board
- ☐ straight pins
- ☐ photocopies of the handout (p. 106)
- ☐ bath tissue tube for each child
- ☐ chenille wires
- ☐ wrapping paper
- ☐ tape
- ☐ small wrapped candies
- ☐ safety scissors

A Powerful Purpose

Preschool children will give thanks, as the pilgrims did, for blessings in their lives.

A Look at the Lesson

1. God Loves Me Every Day
2. Chalk Drawings
3. Shake a Story
4. Pat a Pilgrims' Prayer
5. Friendship Feast
6. Seeds Are Beautiful
7. We Give Thanks
8. We Thank God
9. God's Gifts
10. Great Growth Charts
11. God's Love Keeps Growing

Young children are interested *in doing things with their friends. They also love to hear stories—especially stories that happened long ago or "once upon a time..."*

Use this lesson to help preschoolers learn about Thanksgiving. Give them an opportunity to thank God for blessings in their lives.

The Lively Lesson

1. God Loves Me Every Day

Greet the children, then gather in a circle. Tell them they're going to learn about Thanksgiving and have a chance to give thanks for their blessings.

Teach children this song to the tune of "Twinkle, Twinkle, Little Star." Have them repeat, line by line with actions, then slowly combine all lines together.

I know God loves me every day. (Hug self.)
God shows me in many ways (arms extended, separated slightly, palms up):
My family and my friends he gave (hands over heart),
And the good food that I eat. (Touch lips.)

God's good blessings with me stay. *(Arms raised, palms open.)*

I know God loves me every day. *(Hug self.)*

2. Chalk Drawings

(You'll need sidewalk chalk.)

Take children outside to make chalk drawings on a sidewalk. If that's not an option, have them make chalk drawings on a sheet of paper. Have kids each draw a picture representing something they're thankful for. As they do, encourage them to thank God for the good things in their life.

Say: **The pilgrims were a group of people who remembered to thank God, just as you did when you drew your pictures. Let's hear why they were thankful.**

3. Shake a Story

(Pour the cold heavy whipping cream into the see-through container with a tight-fitting lid. Shake the container for five to six minutes to begin the butter-making process. Kids will continue to shake during the activity—approximately two to three more minutes.)

Pass around the container filled with heavy whipping cream. Explain that the kids will take turns shaking the container to make butter while you tell the story of the pilgrims.

Once upon a time, long ago, the pilgrims came to America. These people came from across the sea. When they got here, though, they didn't know how to grow foods in a new land. So the Indians showed them how to grow things like corn, pumpkins, and beans and how to prepare and eat turkey. Without the Indians' help, the pilgrims would have had little to eat and would have starved.

The first year, when all the foods were ready to eat, the pilgrims had a big feast and invited their Indian friends. They thanked God for all the delicious new foods and for their new friends. And each Thanksgiving Day, we do the same thing when we thank God for food, friends, families, and all the gifts God gives us.

Today we'll celebrate our own Friendship Feast with the butter you've just been making. Let's thank God for our butter and all our blessings.

Set the forming butter aside.

4. Pat a Pilgrims' Prayer

Ask kids to pat their knees in rhythm. Tell them they're going to pat a prayer to a one-two beat. Ask the kids to repeat each line after you say it. Keep the patting rhythm going throughout the prayer.

**Thank you, God,
For these gifts:
Food,
Families,
Friends,
Our beautiful earth,
Us,
Jesus.
He sure loves us.
He calls us friends.
In Jesus' name,
Amen!**

5. Friendship Feast

(You'll need a Bible, the butter, crackers, a bowl, a butter knife, chocolate milk, napkins, and cups.)

Help the children remove the lid from the container. Pour off the liquid into the empty bowl. Spread butter on crackers. Also serve chocolate milk or another drink kids will be thankful for.

Say: **There's a Bible verse that's nice for Thanksgiving. Listen to it as you eat your crackers and butter.**

Read Psalm 107:1 from a children's Bible, or use this version: **"Give thanks to the Lord, for he is good! His faithful love endures forever."**

6. Seeds Are Beautiful

(Copy a "We Are Thankful" handout from page 106 onto construction paper for each child. You'll also need glue and seeds.)

Tell kids they're going to make seed pictures by gluing seeds onto the handout. Older kids may want to glue seeds in the shape of the earth, their friends, their families, their pets, their churches, their homes, or whatever they're thankful for. Others may want to create a free design. Let the children glue seeds on their handout in any way they choose.

Say: **Seeds are one thing to thank God for. We can use them for food or plant them to grow more food.**

7. We Give Thanks

(You'll need straight pins and a bulletin board titled "We Give Thanks.")

Gather in a circle. Ask the children each to show their picture and explain what they're thankful for. Pin the pictures to the bulletin board titled "We Give Thanks." Read the bulletin board title to the kids.

8. We Thank God

Sing the following song to the tune of "Three Blind Mice." As you sing things pictured on the bulletin board, encourage kids to point them out.

> We thank God.
> We thank God.
> For he is good.
> For he is good!
> God gives beautiful
> Gifts to us.
> He gives us families
> That love us so much.
> He gives us food, friends,
> And a wonderful life,
> So we thank God.

9. God's Gifts

(You'll need a bath tissue tube for each child, chenille wires, wrapping paper, tape, small wrapped candies, and safety scissors.)

Say: **Let's make gifts to take home to our families.**

Give each child a bath tissue tube and a piece of wrapping paper. Show children how to wrap and tape the tube in the wrapping paper, leaving wrapping paper extending past the tube on both ends. Then show children how to cinch and tie one end of the wrapping paper closed with a chenille wire. Give kids each a few pieces of wrapped candy to put in the tube, and help them tie the other end closed with a chenille wire.

Say: **Give this gift to someone in your family. Tell about the good gifts God gives us.**

10. Great Growth Charts

(Make growth charts by cutting 6x24-inch butcher paper strips, one for each child. With a marker, mark 1-inch measurements along the side. Start at the bottom with 24 inches and go up to 48 inches. You'll also need crayons.)

Say: **Food is not the only thing that grows. What else grows that we're thankful for?** Pause for answers.

There are lots of things that grow. Even you! Now we're going to make a growth chart so you can measure how much you grow.

Give each child a growth chart prepared earlier. Let kids each decorate their chart to take home and hang on a wall.

Help them measure their present height. Tell kids to thank God for his measureless, endless love each time they measure their growth.

11. God's Love Keeps Growing

(You'll need the completed growth charts.)
Ask children to bring their completed growth charts and gather in a circle. For a closing prayer, begin with: **Thanks, God, for your love that keeps growing…** Have kids, one at a time, say "and growing" as they hold up their growth chart. Continue around the circle so each child has a chance to add to the prayer. When it gets back to you, say: **In Jesus' name, amen!**

"We Are Thankful"

"Give thanks to the Lord, for he is good!
His faithful love endures forever"
(Psalm 107:1).

Christmas Celebration

A Powerful Purpose

Preschool children will relate their own experiences with babies to the baby Jesus of long ago.

A Sprinkling of Supplies

- ☐ Bible
- ☐ diaper
- ☐ baby rattles
- ☐ baby powder
- ☐ ointment
- ☐ booties
- ☐ receiving blanket
- ☐ spoons
- ☐ napkins
- ☐ photocopies of the handout (p. 111)
- ☐ scrap fabric cut in strips
- ☐ crayons
- ☐ glue sticks
- ☐ pots
- ☐ pans
- ☐ lids
- ☐ spoons
- ☐ bowls
- ☐ applesauce in baby food jars
- ☐ paper plates
- ☐ popcorn kernels
- ☐ stapler
- ☐ markers
- ☐ sponges
- ☐ scissors
- ☐ paper
- ☐ paint
- ☐ shallow pans

A Look at the Lesson

1. Baby Song
2. Baby Hide-and-Seek
3. What Do You Know About Babies?
4. Action-Packed Story
5. Snackin' Time
6. Jesus' Birthday
7. Sponge Painting
8. Wrapping Baby Jesus
9. Rattle Rhymes
10. Musical Maracas
11. Christmas Sing-Along
12. Christmas Prayer

Babies, babies everywhere. All of us were once babies. The Christmas story tells of Jesus' birth and the miraculous events surrounding the beginning of this special baby's life.

Use this lesson to show similarities and differences between babies now and the baby Jesus on the first Christmas.

The Lively Lesson

1. Baby Song

Welcome the children, and say: **We all used to be babies once. Did you know that Jesus was a little baby once, too? Let's learn a song about what a special baby Jesus was.** Sing the following song to the tune of "Did You Ever See a Lassie?"

When Jesus was a baby *(pretend to rock a baby),*
A baby, a baby *(pretend to rock a baby),*
When Jesus was a baby *(pretend to rock a baby),*
He laughed and he cried. *(Smile and then wipe eyes.)*

He laughed and he cried. *(Smile and then wipe eyes.)*
He laughed and he cried. *(Smile and then wipe eyes.)*
When Jesus was a baby *(pretend to rock a baby),*
He laughed and he cried. *(Smile and then wipe eyes.)*

2. Baby Hide-and-Seek

(On a table place a diaper, baby rattle, baby powder, ointment, booties, and one receiving blanket.)

Gather the children around the table. Say: **Today we're talking about babies. And we're going to learn about a special baby—Jesus.**

Discuss the items on the table and how they're used for babies. Then cover the items with the receiving blanket. Ask children to cover their eyes while you remove one item. Uncover the items, and see if children can name the missing one. Play this game several times, but quit before children lose interest.

3. What Do You Know About Babies?

Gather in a circle, sit down, and discuss:
• How many of you have a baby in your home?
• How many of you have played with a baby?
• What do babies do?
• Where are babies born?
• What can you tell me about Jesus when he was a baby?
• What do we call the special day when Jesus was born?

Say: **Babies do all kinds of things. They giggle.** Ask kids to giggle. **They cry.** Ask kids to pretend to cry. **They like to be hugged.** Tell kids each to hug the people sitting on both sides of them.

Jesus was a baby, too. He giggled, cried, and liked to be hugged. He was born long ago in a town called Bethlehem. We celebrate Jesus' birthday on Christmas.

4. Action-Packed Story

Ask children to stand. Lead them in the following action-packed Christmas story.

Joseph and Mary had to take a trip on a donkey. *(Walk in place; pretend to pull a stubborn donkey.)*
Joseph and Mary looked for a place to stay. *(Look around, up high, down low, under things.)*
The innkeeper had no room for them. *(Shake head.)*
Mary and Joseph slept on the stable floor. *(Lie on the floor.)*
When Jesus was born, they wrapped him up. *(Pretend to wrap a baby and cuddle him.)*
Mary laid him in a manger. *(Pretend to lay baby down.)*
Mary and Joseph thanked God. *(Fold hands, look to heaven.)*

5. Snackin' Time

(You'll need applesauce—served in baby food jars if possible, spoons, and napkins.)

Ask kids to follow you to a snack table. March to this chant:
Time, time, time to eat.
Follow me to a little treat!

As children enjoy the applesauce, have them think about babies who eat real baby food from jars.

6. Jesus' Birthday

(You'll need a children's Bible.)
Tell children to continue eating their snack

and listen to a story about the very first Christmas. Read Luke 2:1-20.

Ask:
- **What town was Jesus born in?**
- **Where did he sleep?**
- **What did he wear?**

Say: **Jesus was born in a place where they kept animals—something like a barn. His bed was a manger—what they used to hold food for animals. He wore cloths that wrapped all around him to keep him warm.**

7. Sponge Painting

(You'll need sponges, scissors, paper, and paint in shallow pans.)

Before class, cut sponges into Christmas shapes such as an angel, star, and baby. Or you can buy shaped sponges at your local craft store.

Show children how to dip the sponges into the paint. Let kids sponge paint as they share what they remember about Jesus' birth from the Bible story.

8. Wrapping Baby Jesus

(You'll need the "Baby Jesus" handout from page 111, scrap fabric cut in strips, crayons, and glue sticks.)

Ask kids to follow you to the table with the supplies. Tell them they're going to remember that first Christmas—baby Jesus' birthday—by wrapping Jesus in swaddling clothes.

Give each child a "Baby Jesus" handout. Have them each color baby Jesus' face. Then help them each glue the fabric strips to Jesus' body.

9. Rattle Rhymes

(You'll need one baby rattle for each child. Church nurseries usually have plenty.)

Give children each a baby rattle. Read the following word groups. In each group, have the children listen for the word that relates to Jesus' birth. When they hear one, kids should shake their rattles. Do the first one or two with them.

Ball, <u>baby,</u> bubble
Bowl, bicycle, <u>Bethlehem</u>
Caterpillar, <u>Christmas,</u> cartwheel
Minnie, Mollie, <u>Mary</u>
Monkey, <u>manger,</u> Montana
<u>God,</u> golf, green

Say: **Jesus was a real baby, a lot like babies you've seen. And he is also God. He came to earth as a baby and then grew up to save us from our sins.**

10. Musical Maracas

(You'll need paper plates, popcorn kernels, a stapler, and markers.)

Say: **Let's sing some Christmas songs as we think about Jesus coming to earth as a baby. But first, we need to make instruments to help us create beautiful music.**

Demonstrate how to make a maraca by placing popcorn kernels on a paper plate. Help children staple another paper plate over the top of the first plate. Then give children time to decorate their maracas with markers.

11. Christmas Sing-Along

(You'll need the maracas from the previous activity, plus pots, pans, lids, spoons, and bowls—anything that can be used as a musical instrument.)

Invite children to use their maracas or the pots and pans to beat a rhythm. For example, kids can shake their maracas, hit two lids together, click two spoons together, or use a spoon to tap on a bowl or pan.

Sing some of the kids' favorite Christmas songs such as "Away in a Manger" and "Joy to the World." Direct the instrumentalists to play as they sing.

12. Christmas Prayer

Ask kids to hold their instruments quietly as you pray. You'll signal them to "make a joyful noise" at the end of the prayer.

Pray: **Thanks for babies, God. Thanks especially for baby Jesus and his birthday—Christmas. In Jesus' name, amen.**

Ask kids to play their instruments as they shout "Merry Christmas!" Let children take their maracas home.

Baby Jesus

The Savior has been born in Bethlehem!
(adapted from Luke 2:11)

Permission to copy this handout from *Lively Bible Lessons for MOPPETS* granted for local church use.
Copyright © Group Publishing, Inc., P.O. Box 481, Loveland, CO 80539. www.group.com

For more **amazing resources**

visit us at
group.com...

...or call us at
1-800-447-1070

Also available at your favorite Christian Retailer.

Group
Incredible things will happen